10·20·30 MINUTES TO QUILT

NANCY ZIEMAN

Oxmoor House®

10•20•30 Minutes to Quilt
by Nancy Zieman
from the "Sewing with Nancy" series
©2000 by Nancy Zieman and Oxmoor House, Inc.
Book Division of Southern Progress Corporation
2100 Lakeshore Drive, Birmingham, Alabama 35209

Published by Oxmoor House, Inc., and Leisure Arts, Inc.

Library of Congress Catalog Number: 99-85953
Hardcover ISBN: 0-8487-2368-6
Softcover ISBN: 0-8487-2371-6
Printed in the United States of America
First Printing 2000

Editor-in-Chief: Nancy Fitzpatrick Wyatt
Senior Crafts Editor: Susan Ramey Cleveland
Senior Editor, Editorial Services: Olivia Kindig Wells
Art Director: James Boone

10•20•30 Minutes to Quilt
Editors: Rhonda Richards, Catherine Corbett Fowler
Copy Editor: L. Amanda Owens
Editorial Assistant: Suzanne Powell
Associate Art Director: Cynthia R. Cooper
Senior Designer/Illustrator: Emily Albright Parrish
Director, Production and Distribution: Phillip Lee
Associate Production Manager: Larry Hunter
Senior Photographer: John O'Hagan
Photo Stylists: Kathy Harris, Linda Baltzell Wright
Illustrator: Kelly Davis

Contributors
Proofreader: Laura Morris Edwards
Illustrator: Laure Noe

We're Here for You!
We at Oxmoor House are dedicated to serving you with reliable information that expands your
imagination and enriches your life. We welcome your comments and suggestions.
Please write us at:
Oxmoor House, Inc.
Editor, *10•20•30 Minutes to Quilt*
2100 Lakeshore Drive
Birmingham, AL 35209
To order additional publications, call 1-800-633-4910.

Thanks to Heart to Heart Quilt Shop and Sew Bizz in Trussville, Alabama, for use
of their shops and Pfaff sewing machines/sergers for photography.

Contents

Quilting Essentials

BEFORE YOU BEGIN QUILTING, THERE ARE A FEW NECESSITIES TO

GATHER. Modern products make quick work of what once took hours to complete.

So with the right supplies at your fingertips, you really can get a lot done, even when

you have just 10, 20, or 30 minutes to spare.

HAVING THE PROPER TOOLS WILL ALSO INCREASE YOUR

ENJOYMENT OF QUILTING AND IMPROVE YOUR ACCURACY. New products

are constantly appearing on the market, but on the following pages, you'll find a list of

must-haves to get you started.

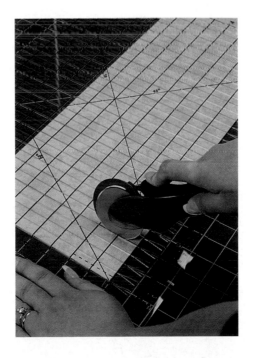

ROTARY CUTTER

Instead of individually cutting out pieces of fabric with scissors, the modern quilter uses the rotary cutter to cut many pieces at a time through multiple layers of fabric.

Dritz® has further refined the rotary cutter by developing tools that automatically close when not in use. Until now, there was a danger of cutting yourself if you inadvertently placed your cutter on the table without closing it. Dritz eliminates that risk: the blade is exposed only as you bear down on the cutter to cut fabric. For extra protection, switch the cutter to a "locked" position when not in use; or control how much of the blade is revealed by selecting "light" or "heavy duty."

CUTTING MAT

Purchase the largest mat you can afford, making sure it measures at least 18" x 22" (45 cm x 55 cm). A self-healing mat is designed for use with the rotary cutter.

CUTTING RULERS

The longer you quilt, the more rulers you will buy. Start with a 6" x 24" (15 cm x 61 cm) ruler; later you may want to add 6"-square (15 cm-square), 12½"-square (31.25 cm), and triangle rulers. I'll introduce you to other specialty cutting rulers that will help you with particular projects.

JUNE TAILOR SHAPE CUT PLUS

A new quilter often finds that the ruler slips or that the rotary cutter strays from the ruler edge. The Shape Cut Plus eliminates this problem. This large ruler has grooves cut within it at ½" (1.25 cm) and 1" (2.5 cm) intervals. When strip cutting, use this tool to cut long strips accurately.

Rotary Cutter

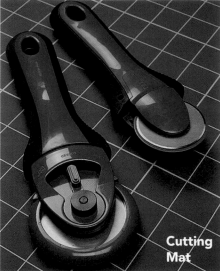

Cutting Mat

June Tailor Shape Cut Plus

CUTTING TABLE

Your worktable should be a comfortable height at which to stand while you cut and work. Most people prefer a table about 36" (91.5 cm) high. Some tables have collapsible sides to conserve space when not in use.

THREAD CLIPPERS

Trim threads easily with this spring-action tool. Keep this handy item by your sewing machine to snip threads quickly without having to insert your fingers into the scissor handles.

FABRIC SHEARS

A fine pair of sharp fabric shears will become one of your treasured possessions. To keep them sharp, do not cut anything but fabric with them.

PAPER SCISSORS

Use an inexpensive pair of large, sharp scissors to cut freezer paper and paper patterns—everything except fabric. Let your family know that if they borrow a pair of scissors from your work space, borrow these!

STEAM IRON

Look for a steam iron that produces plenty of steam, like the one below from Rowenta®. The iron's generous burst of steam lets you flatten seams and remove stubborn creases. Its soleplate has a tough no-scratch surface.

Steam Iron

Cutting Table, Sides Down

Cutting Table, Open

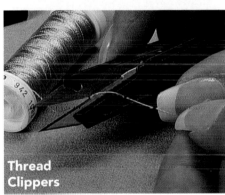

Thread Clippers

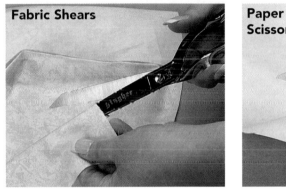

Fabric Shears

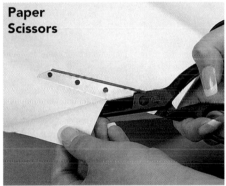

Paper Scissors

SEWING MACHINE

If you spend a considerable amount of time at your sewing machine, you'll want a high-quality machine that makes piecing a breeze. I use a Pfaff 7570, which has an exclusive dual feed (that means I never have to attach a walking foot for things like machine quilting). In addition, it has a needle-down feature, an automatic needle threader, and over 200 built-in decorative stitches. I can also hook it up to my home computer, which creates nearly endless design possibilities. It's like having a sewing machine, a quilting machine, and an embroidery machine all in one.

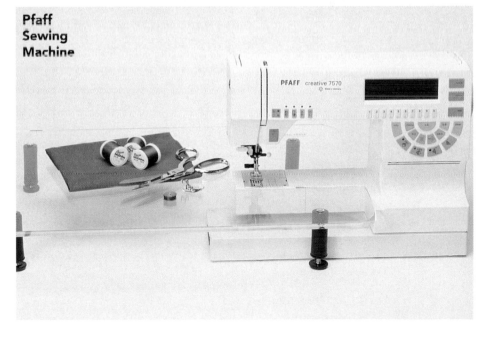

Pfaff Sewing Machine

LITTLE FOOT®

This foot is essential in quiltmaking. The right edge of the Little Foot is ¼" (0.6 cm) from the center needle position, making it ideal for machine piecing. The wider left toe—⅜" (1 cm) from the needle—provides better fabric feed control, especially on newer machines with a wider distance between the feed dogs. It features ¼" (0.6 cm) notches in front of and behind the center needle position that are perfect references for starting, stopping, and pivoting.

BIG FOOT®

Use the Big Foot for free-motion machine quilting. It provides more surface contact with the fabric "sandwich" than traditional feet. The clear plastic foot gives you excellent visibility, letting you see where you're going and where you've been.

DUAL MARKING PEN

Dritz makes a dual-end marking pen for drawing quilting designs on fabric. The water-erasable end makes bright blue marks that are easily removed with plain water. The air-erasable end makes bright purple marks that vanish in 12 to 24 hours without washing. The pen makes fine lines so that you can trace small designs or mark complex patterns clearly.

CURVED BASTING PINS

For pin-basting quilts, these safety pins have the correct angle for easy, comfortable insertion into the quilt sandwich. The pins are nickel-plated brass and are guaranteed not to rust. The pins can remain safely in the quilt until the project is complete. Use the size 1 pin for low-loft projects and the size 2 pin when making quilts with a thick batting.

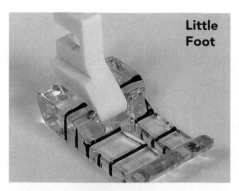

Little Foot

Big Foot

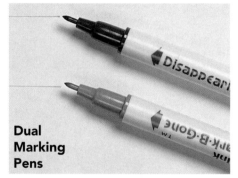

Dual Marking Pens

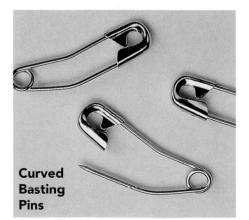

Curved Basting Pins

MACHINE-QUILTING NEEDLES

Schmetz's machine-quilting needles are ideal for machine-quilting with cotton thread. Designed with a special taper to the point, these needles will successfully sew thick layers of cross seams in any quilting or patchwork project. If you enjoy free-form quilting, you'll want the version with an attached spring.

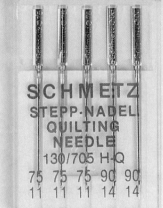

Machine-Quilting Needles

TIGER TAPE™

Those who do hand stitching take pride in the uniformity of their stitches. Tiger Tape helps you evenly space your stitches. The adhesive-backed tape is available in two widths. The ¼" (0.6 cm) width is marked with either four lines or nine lines per inch; the ¹⁄₁₆" (0.15 cm) has nine lines per inch. Position the reusable tape next to the stitching line on your project and then sew a stitch at every line, at every other line, or at any interval you prefer.
• Use the ¼" (0.6 cm) width for outline quilting.
• Use the flexible ¹⁄₁₆" (0.15 cm) width for gentle curves.

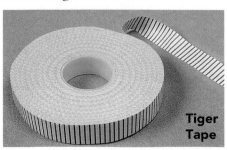

Tiger Tape

LASER II® QUILTER'S BASTING GUN AND QUILTER'S BASTING GRATE

HOW TO USE A BASTING GUN

1. Tie long strings (longer than the quilt dimension) to the four corners of the Quilter's Basting Grate *(Diagram A).* These strings let you move the grate and reposition it during the tack-basting process.

2. Place the grate on a flat surface (a table or perhaps the floor for a large quilt). Place the backing over the grate; tape the backing securely to the flat surface, with the wrong side up *(Diagram B)*. Using the strings, move the grate to the center of the backing.

3. Layer the batting and the quilt top (with the right side up) over the quilt back, making certain all the layers are wrinkle free.

4. Place a pin in the center of the quilt to hold all the layers together *(Diagram C).*

5. Load the plastic strip of tacks into the Basting Gun, following the package instructions. $\longrightarrow$

Traditionally, quilters have hand basted the layers of a quilt together. While this is still a popular option, there are new tools available that can make this work much faster, plus allow you to easily baste a quilt right on your own tabletop.

The lightweight Laser II Quilter's Basting Gun temporarily "staples" layers together, using a fine needle to insert extralong ⅜" (1 cm) plastic tacks. It's similar to the tool used to attach price tags to garments in retail stores.

The Quilter's Basting Grate slips under the layered quilt and allows room to easily staple the layers together. After you finish quilting, use the Basting Tack Remover to snip tacks away.

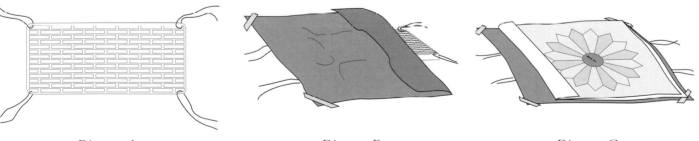

Diagram A   Diagram B   Diagram C

CORNER MARK-IT™

6. Be sure the grate is under the area you are basting. Press the nose of the gun firmly against the fabric, making certain the needle is totally inserted through all layers of the quilt before pulling the trigger and withdrawing the needle *(Diagram D)*. Because the needle is very fine, it will not make a mark in the fabric. Space additional tacks 3" to 4" (7.5 cm to 10 cm) apart.

7. Baste the entire quilt, repositioning the grate under the quilt back as needed, using the strings.

8. After hand- or machine-quilting the quilt, remove the tacks by sliding the Basting Tack Remover along the fabric to cut the tacks in one easy motion *(Diagram E)*. Or carefully clip the tacks with scissors, taking care not to cut the quilt fabric.

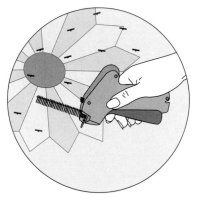

Diagram D

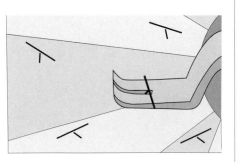

Diagram E

In the past, a tracing wheel was a marking mainstay. Today, quilters can choose from countless marking tools, including the Corner Mark-It™. Here's how to apply binding with smoothly mitered corners.

1. Prepare the binding strips.

• For a double-fold binding with a finished width of ½" (1.3 cm), cut crosswise strips 2½" (6.3 cm) wide.

• For each edge to be bound, cut the needed length plus 3" (7.5 cm) *(Diagram A)*. If necessary, piece the strips together.

• Fold and press the binding strips in half, matching the wrong sides of the lengthwise edges.

2. On the wrong side of the quilt, mark the starting and stopping points ¼" (0.6 cm) from each corner, using the small pencil hole on the top left corner of the Corner Mark-It *(Diagram B)*.

3. Working with the wrong side of the quilt up, pin the first binding strip on the right side of the quilt, leaving a 1½" (3.8 cm) tail at each end *(Diagram C)*.

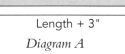

Diagram A

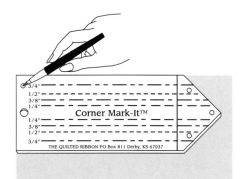

Diagram B

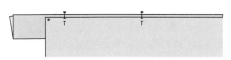

Diagram C

4. Sew the binding to the quilt, using a ¼" (0.6 cm) seam allowance; stop and start on the marked dot and lock stitches at each dot *(Diagram D)*. Repeat for the remaining three sides of the quilt, pulling the previous binding strip out of the way so that it is not caught in the stitching.

5. Turn the quilt over. Mark the corner miter.

• Place the Corner Mark-It on one end of a binding strip, with the upper marked ½" (1.3 cm) line (representing the finished width of the binding) over the stitched seam. The corresponding finished width line at the lower edge of the Corner Mark-It will be at the fold of the binding *(Diagram E)*.

• Slide the Corner Mark-It until the angled end meets the starting/stopping point of the stitching. Mark around the end *(Diagram F)*.

6. With the wrong sides together, fold the quilt diagonally at the corner, with adjacent bindings on top of each other. Carefully align the raw edges. Stitch on the marked V line, using a short stitch length and fastening the threads at each end *(Diagram G)*. Trim the seam allowances.

7. Turn the corner right side out, using a Bamboo Pointer and Creaser *(Diagram H)*.

8. On the back of the quilt, position the folded edge of the binding so that it covers the stitching line *(Diagram I)*. Hand-sew the binding in place.

BINDING & HEM CLIPS

Binding and hem clips hold quilt bindings firmly in place while you stitch. The clips stay put until you remove them. The 1¾" (4.5 cm) clips are rust-proof nickel-plated steel.

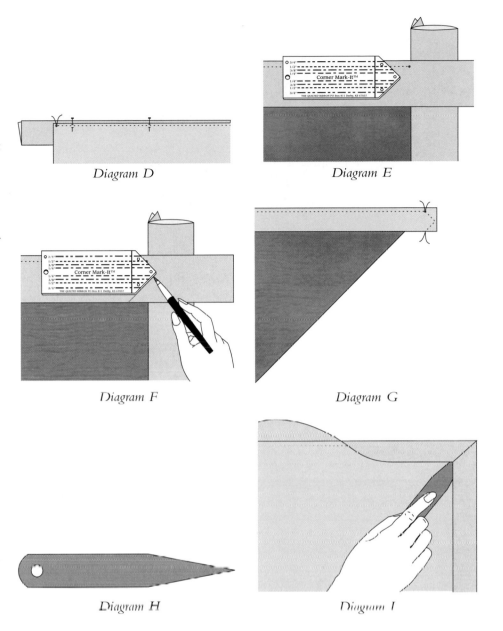

Diagram D

Diagram E

Diagram F

Diagram G

Diagram H

Diagram I

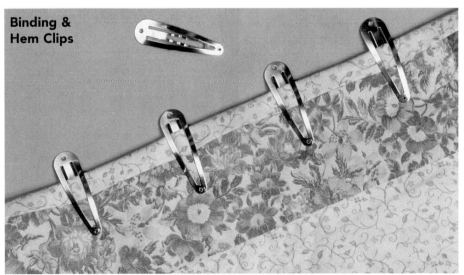

Binding & Hem Clips

2
Playful Patchwork

If you've ever pieced fabrics into patchwork designs—or even if you've contemplated doing so—you may not have considered that process playful. Yet, as I experimented with various designs and projects, I became increasingly energetic and enthusiastic. The art of sewing definitely is dynamic when it involves patchwork!

I'VE FOUND THAT USING STRIP SETS OR STRATA (FABRIC STRIPS STITCHED TOGETHER AND RECUT INTO SECTIONS) REALLY SIMPLIFIES PATCHWORK. I'll show you the basics and then explain how to make some specific projects, such as a Roman Stripe baby quilt, a Kaleidoscope Quilt, and a Trip Around the World pillow.

Squares are the springboard to some other playful patchwork variations. I shaped them into a *Four-Patch* quilt, a *Rail Fence* throw, and a *Radiating Squares* wall hanging. They're all fast and fun!

I'M CONFIDENT YOU'LL FIND PATCHWORK AS STIMULATING AND INVIGORATING AS I DO. Have fun piecing—and playing—with patchwork!

Strip-Piecing Basics

A STRIP SET (FABRIC STRIPS STITCHED TOGETHER AND THEN RECUT
INTO SECTIONS) IS THE BASIS FOR MANY PATCHWORK DESIGNS. LET'S START
WITH THE BASICS AND CREATE A STRIP SET.

PREPARING STRATA

1. Select two contrasting or coordinating fabrics.

• Label one fabric "dark."

• Label the second fabric "light."

2. Cut each fabric into 45" (115 cm) crosswise strips.

• The strip width determines the size of the completed design. Generally, for the projects included in this book, cut the strips 1" to 3" (2.5 cm to 7.5 cm) wide.

• Prepare the fabric for cutting.

- Fold the fabric in half, meeting the selvage edges.

- Fold the fabric again, bringing the fold to the selvages (*Diagram A*). (There will be four layers of fabric.)

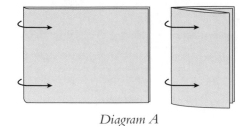
Diagram A

- Place the fabric on a rotary cutting mat, aligning the fold along one of the horizontal lines at the lower edge of the mat.

- Position a ruler on the fabric, perpendicular to the fold, to form a right angle. Straighten the fabric edge and use a rotary cutter to trim any excess fabric (*Diagram B*).

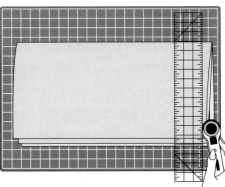
Diagram B

• Cut the strips to the desired size.

- Align one of the ruler's horizontal lines with the fabric fold. Working from the straightened edge, place the line corresponding to the desired strip width along the straightened edge of the fabric.

- Cut three strips from each fabric, using a rotary cutter (*Diagram C*).

3. Stitch the strips into strip sets.

• Form two groupings, each containing three strips (*Diagram D*).

- For one grouping, position a dark strip in the center of two

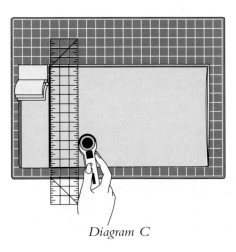
Diagram C

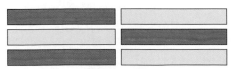
Diagram D

light strips.

- For the second grouping, position a light strip in the center of two dark strips.

• Set the stitch length to 12 stitches per inch (2.5), slightly shorter than usual. Because the strips will be recut, a shorter stitch length makes stitching more secure.

• Join the lengthwise edges of each grouping with ¼" (0.6 cm) seams, with the right sides together. *(Note: All projects in this book use ¼" [0.6 cm] seams.)*

> *Note from Nancy:* To achieve accurate ¼" (0.6 cm) seams, I like to use the Little Foot™. The right toe of the foot is exactly ¼" (0.6 cm) wide. If I position the right edge of the foot along the cut edges of my strips, I get precise, uniform seams every time. The left edge of the foot is a scant ⅜" (1 cm) from the center needle position, giving better tension control.

4. Press the seams in one of these ways (*Diagram E*, top of page 17):

• The quickest way is to press each seam in one direction, generally toward the darker fabric. This is the approach traditionally used in quilting.

• For greater accuracy, press each seam open. This takes slightly more time but distributes the bulk more evenly and makes it easy to match seam intersections. This technique is especially appropriate if both fabrics are of the same intensity so that there is no show-through.

5. Cut each strip set into sections.

• Straighten the edge of the strip set as detailed in Step 2, aligning the ruler's horizontal markings with the cut edge of the strips.

• Cut the strip set sections at the same width as the original strip size. For example, if the original strips were 2" (5 cm) wide, then cut the sections 2" (5 cm) wide *(Diagram F)*.

• Separate the cut sections into two groupings *(Diagram G)*, with those of each color grouping together. Cut six sections of one coloration and seven sections of the other.

6. Chainstitch pairs together.

• Meet one section of each coloration, with the right sides together.

• Join the sections with a ¼" (0.6 cm) seam. Do not raise the presser foot or cut the threads.

• Butt the next pair of cut sections to the first pair; continue stitching *(Diagram H)*.

• Chainstitch six pairs together, following the same process.

• Cut between each of the stitched pairs.

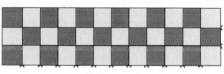

For speed: press seam in one direction.   For accuracy: press open.

Diagram E

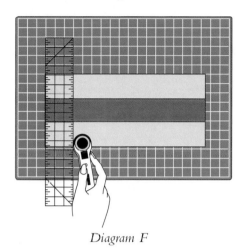

Diagram F

7. Join the six pairs into a long rectangle, alternating colorations *(Diagram I)*.

• Add a single section at the end. (a total of thirteen sections will be sewn together.)

• Press the seams open.

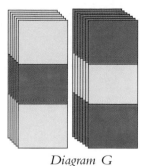

Diagram G

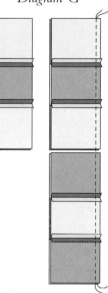

Diagram H

Diagram I

SPECIALTY RULERS FOR CUTTING STRIP SETS

Since specialty rulers can simplify cutting for many projects, you'll want to add them to your collection as you stitch more quilts. The Kaleidoscope Wedge Ruler™ by Marilyn Doheny, for example, makes it easy to cut accurate pie-shaped pieces for the Kaleidoscope Quilt featured on page 26. See Resources on page 144 for ordering information.

Rail Fence

THIS QUILTED THROW SHOWCASES A RAIL FENCE DESIGN.
RATHER THAN WORKING WITH INDIVIDUAL PIECES FOR EACH PORTION OF
THE FENCE, STITCH A FIVE-STRIP SET AND THEN CUT THE SEWN STRIPS
INTO SQUARES. IT'S AN EFFORTLESS, BASIC TECHNIQUE THAT
IS THE SPRINGBOARD TO OTHER PLAYFUL PATCHWORK VARIATIONS.

**Quilt designed by Nancy
Zieman; pieced by
Patricia Everman Myers;
quilted by New Traditions**

Finished Size (without borders):
37½" x 37½" (95.3 cm x 95.3 cm)
Blocks: 7½" (19.3 cm)

Note from Nancy: The Rail
Fence traditionally uses three strips,
with each strip making a step design.
Our variation uses five strips; only the
outer strips make the step design. You
could apply the same technique to
strip sets containing three to six strips.

MATERIALS

⅓ yard (0.32 m) each of five fabrics,
  ranging from light to dark
1 yard (0.95 m) fabric for borders
  and binding
⅛ (0.15 m) yard fabric (or 4 [3½"
  or 9 cm] squares) accent fabric for
  corner squares
1⅜ yards (1.30 m) fabric for backing
Twin-size batting

CUTTING
 10 Minutes

Measurements include ¼" (0.6 cm)
seam allowances. Cut crosswise strips
unless otherwise noted.
From each of the five fabrics, cut:
• Five 2"-wide (5 cm–wide) strips
  for strip sets.
From the border fabric, cut:
• Four 3½"-wide (9 cm–wide) strips
  for borders.
• Five 2¼"-wide (5.6 cm–wide)
  strips for binding.

BLOCK ASSEMBLY
⏱ 30 Minutes ⏱

1. Join five 2"-wide (5 cm-wide) strips to form a strip set, as detailed on pages 16 and 17.

2. Press the seam allowances open.

3. Measure the width of the stip set. Using this measurement, cut the strip set into squares *(Diagram A).* (A five-strip set of 2" [5 cm] strips should measure 8" [20.5 cm] wide. The strip set width may vary if a wider or narrower seam allowance was used. Cut the square to whatever width the strip set measures.) Cut sufficient squares to make the desired size quilt. Our design used 25 (7½" or 19.3 cm, finished-size) squares.

QUILT ASSEMBLY
⏱ 30 Minutes ⏱

1. Arrange the cut squares into the Rail Fence pattern as follows.

• First row: Alternate the horizontal and vertical squares, starting with a horizontal square.

• Second row: Alternate the squares, starting with a vertical square *(Diagram B).*

• Repeat the sequence in subsequent rows, alternating the horizontal and vertical squares *(Diagram C).*

2. Join the blocks into rows. Press the seam allowances in opposite directions.

3. Join the rows to complete the quilt center.

⏱ 10 Minutes ⏱

4. Measure the length of the quilt. Trim four borders to this measurement. Add a border to each quilt side.

5. Sew an accent square to each end of the remaining borders. Add the borders to the quilt top and bottom *(Diagram D).*

QUILTING & FINISHING

1. Layer the backing (facedown), the batting, and the quilt top (faceup). Baste the layers together.

2. Quilt as desired. The quilt shown was machine-quilted in an allover tropical fish design.

3. Join 2¼"-wide (5.6 cm-wide) strips into one continous piece to make binding. Add the binding.

Diagram A

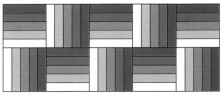

Diagram B

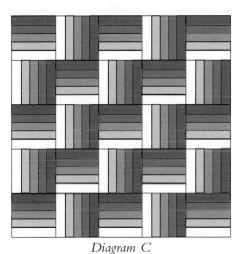

Diagram C

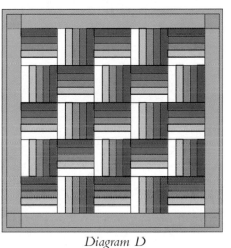

Diagram D

Roman Stripe Baby Quilt

SUPERSIMPLE SEWING CREATES THIS COLORFUL BABY QUILT. THE DESIGN
IS FORMED BY ALTERNATING COLORATIONS AND POSITIONING QUILT BLOCKS
IN OPPOSITE DIRECTIONS. SOFT HAND-DYED FABRICS ADD TO THE QUILT'S
SOFTNESS AND VISUAL APPEAL. IT'S A PERFECT BEGINNER'S PROJECT!

**Quilt designed by Nancy
Zieman; pieced by Patricia
Everman Myers; machine-quilted
by New Traditions. Hand-dyed
fabrics are by Alaska Dyeworks
(see Resources on page 144).**

Finished Size: 29½" x 29½"
(74.8 cm x 74.8 cm)
Blocks: 4½" (11.5 cm)

MATERIALS

12 fat eighths★ hand-dyed fabric
1 yard (0.95 m) fabric for backing
Craft-size batting
★Fat eighth = 9" x 22" (23 cm x
56 cm)

CUTTING
 20 Minutes

Measurements include ¼" (0.6 cm)
seam allowances. Cut crosswise strips
unless otherwise noted.
From each fat eighth, cut:
• Three 2"-wide (5 cm-wide) strips for
blocks.
• One 2¼"-wide (5.6 cm-wide)
strip for binding.

BLOCK ASSEMBLY
⊙ 30 Minutes ⊙

1. Place three 2"-wide (5 cm-wide)
strips next to each other, with the first
and third strips being the same color.
2. Sew the strips together to make a
strip set. Press all the seams in one
direction *(Diagram A)*.
3. Repeat to make strip sets from all
the 2"-wide (5 cm-wide) strips.
4. Measure the width of the strip
set. Cut it into squares of that width
(approximately 5" [12.5 cm] square).
Cut four blocks from each strip set
(Diagram B). You will have extra.

QUILT ASSEMBLY
☽ 30 Minutes ☾

1. Referring to the photo below, alternately position blocks vertically and horizontally, arranging the blocks so that colors and flow are pleasing.

2. Stack the blocks from the second column onto the corresponding blocks from the first column, with the right sides together. Pin the edges together.

3. Stack pairs of pinned blocks. Place blocks 1 and 2 at the top and chain-piece *(Diagram C)*.

4. Fold out the top block of each stitched pair so that the right sides face up.

5. Stack the third column blocks over the second column, with the right sides together. Chain-piece vertical seams as detailed above. The blocks and the rows will be joined together as shown in *Diagram D.*

6. Press the seam allowances for the top row in one direction. For the second row, press the seams in the opposite direction. (This helps minimize bulk when seaming blocks.)

7. Match and stitch horizontal seams, with the right sides together, to complete the quilt top.

QUILTING & FINISHING

1. Layer the backing (facedown), the batting, and the quilt top (faceup). Baste the layers together.

2. Quilt as desired. The quilt shown was machine-quilted in an allover duck design.

3. Join 2¼"-wide (5.6 cm-wide) strips into one continous piece to make binding. Add the binding to the quilt.

Diagram A   *Diagram B*

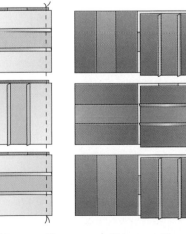

Diagram C   *Diagram D*

Radiating Squares

TAKE A DIFFERENT APPROACH TO FABRIC SQUARES: START WITH
TWO DIFFERENT STRIP SETS, CUT THEM INTO TRIANGLES, AND
REASSEMBLE THEM TO MAKE THE SQUARES THAT SHAPE THIS DRAMATIC
WALL HANGING. YOU'LL LOVE EXPLORING THE POSSIBILITIES!

Quilt by Lois Syens

Finished Size: 35" x 35"
(89 cm x 89 cm)
Blocks: 8¾" (22.5 cm)

MATERIALS

Six ⅓-yard (0.32 m) lengths coordinating prints
1¼ yards (1.15 m) fabric for backing
⅜ yard (0.35 m) fabric for binding
Craft-size batting

CUTTING
🕐 20 Minutes 🕐

Measurements include ¼" (0.6 cm) seam allowances. Cut crosswise strips unless otherwise noted.

From each of the six prints, cut:
• Five 2"-wide (5 cm-wide) strips for strip sets.

From the binding fabric, cut:
• Four 2¼"-wide (5.6 cm-wide) strips for binding.

BLOCK ASSEMBLY
🕐 20 Minutes 🕐

1. Choose three solid fabrics, one each of dark, medium, and light. Choose three print fabrics, one each of dark, medium, and light.

2. Stitch two strip sets *(Diagram A)*.

• Grouping one: light solid, light print, and medium solid.
• Grouping two: medium print, dark solid, and dark print.
• Stitch five strip sets of each grouping. Press the seam allowances open.

🕐 20 Minutes 🕐

3. Cut each strip set into seven triangles.

• Align the 45° angle of a quilting ruler along one outer edge of the strip set, placing the tip of the ruler at the upper left corner. Cut along the ruler, trimming off a 45° angle *(Diagram B)*.

• Flip the ruler from left to right, again aligning the 45° angle with the upper edge of the strip set. Adjust the position of the ruler until the side edge adjacent to the 45° angle aligns at the lower edge with the first cut. This creates a triangle with two 45° angles and one 90° right angle. The sides adjacent to the right angle should be equal in length *(Diagram C)*.

🕐 10 Minutes 🕐

4. Make a template the size of the triangle, using a template material such as Templar®. The templates created from the Templar can be used over and over.

🕐 20 Minutes 🕐

5. Cut additional triangles, flipping the template so that the edge opposite the 90° angle alternately aligns with the top and the bottom of the strip set. On the second strip of that strip set, begin with the long edge of the triangle on the lower edge. Alternate the starting points on each strip to obtain the required number of each coloration *(Diagram D)*.

6. Repeat, cutting triangles from the second strip set.

7. Each strip set produces two different color combinations. (There will be four color combinations.) Stack similar triangles *(Diagram E)*.

🕐 30 Minutes 🕐

8. Join the triangles to make a block.

• Meet two similar triangles, with the right sides together. Stitch a ¼" (0.6 cm) seam along one of the sides perpendicular to the right angle *(Diagram F)*. Chain-piece the remaining triangles into similar pairs. Press the seam allowances open or to one side.

9. Repeat, joining pairs of each of the four colorations. The design requires eight pairs of each coloration, for a total of 32 pairs. ⟶

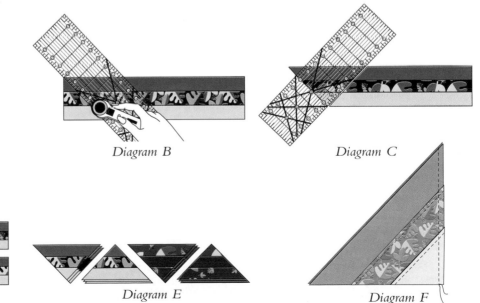

Diagram A

Diagram B

Diagram C

Diagram D

Diagram E

Diagram F

10. Meet two halves to create radiating squares *(Diagram G)*.
• Stitch four squares from the eight pairs of the lightest colorations.
• Stitch four squares from the eight pairs of the darkest colorations.
• Stitch eight squares, each including one triangle of each of the remaining two colorations.

QUILT ASSEMBLY
☾ 30 Minutes ☾

1. Arrange the squares as shown *(Diagram H)*.
• Place the four darkest squares in the center.
• Place the four lightest squares in the corners.
• Fill the remaining spaces with the eight bicolored squares.
2. Stitch the squares together.

QUILTING & FINISHING
1. Layer the backing (facedown), the batting, and the quilt top (faceup). Baste.
2. Quilt as desired. The quilt shown was quilted in a geometric design.
3. Join 2¼"-wide (5.6 cm-wide) strips into one continous piece to make binding. Add the binding *(Diagram I)*.

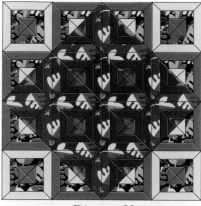

Diagram H

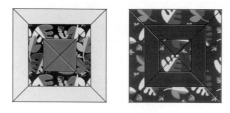

Diagram G

Diagram I

These cool blues, greens, and purples make a lovely accent to a contemporary bedroom or living room. Simply follow the instructions on pages 23 and 24, using three solid fabrics and three prints in a cool color palette rather than in a warm one. Refer to the photo above for placement to make the blocks and to join them into a quilt.

Kaleidoscope Quilt

REMEMBER AS A CHILD BEING FASCINATED WHEN YOU LOOKED THROUGH A KALEIDOSCOPE AND WATCHED THE PATTERNS FORM? THIS QUILTING DESIGN, CREATED BY MARILYN DOHENY, REPRODUCES THAT EFFECT IN FABRIC. THE PATTERN MAY LOOK COMPLEX, BUT IT'S EASY WHEN YOU USE THE KALEIDOSCOPE WEDGE RULER! HERE'S THE SIMPLE TECHNIQUE.

Finished Size: 42" x 42"
(107 cm x 107 cm)
Blocks: 15" (38 cm)

BASIC KALEIDOSCOPE

Choosing fabrics is the first key element in this process. Next, the fabrics are pieced together, cut into wedges, and restitched to produce this unusual effect.

MATERIALS

Choose a favorite color palette as a starting point; then select several fabrics of various values within that color family. It's important to have a range of values to make the completed design distinct. Select:

¾ yard (0.70 m) light fabric for blocks and inner border
½ yard (0.50 m) medium/light fabric for blocks
½ yard (0.50 m) medium/dark fabric for blocks
¾ yard (0.70 m) very dark fabric for blocks and middle border
1 yard (0.95 m) theme print for outer border and binding
1½ yards (1.40 m) fabric for backing
Craft-size batting
Kaleidoscope Wedge Ruler™

CUTTING

🕐 30 Minutes 🕐

From the light fabric, cut:
• Four 2½"-wide (6.3 cm-wide) strips for strip sets.

• Four 1½"-wide (3.8 cm-wide) strips for inner border.

From the medium/light fabric, cut:
• Four 2½"-wide (6.3 cm-wide) strips for strip sets.

From the medium/dark fabric, cut:
• Four 2½"-wide (6.3 cm-wide) strips for strip sets.

From the very dark fabric, cut:
• Four 2½"-wide (6.3 cm-wide) strips for strip sets.
• Four 2½"-wide (6.3 cm-wide) strips for middle border.

From the theme print, cut:
• Four 3½"-wide (9 cm-wide) strips for outer border.
• Five 2¼"-wide (5.6 cm-wide) strips for binding.

BLOCK ASSEMBLY
🕐 20 Minutes 🕐

1. Join all four fabric strips, with the right sides together.
• Arrange 2½"-wide (6.3 cm-wide) strips from light to dark as shown in *Diagram A*.
• Meet the cut edges of the light strip to those of the medium/light strip, with the right sides together. Stitch, using a ¼" (0.6 cm) seam allowance *(Diagram B)*.
• Repeat with the remaining two strips to complete one strip set *(Diagrams C–E)*.
• Repeat to make four strip sets.
• After all the seams are stitched, press all seam allowances in one direction toward the darker fabric. ⟶

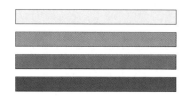

Diagram A

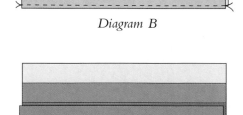

Diagram B

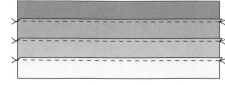

Diagram C

Diagram D

Diagram E

Quilt designed by Marilyn Doheny; pieced by Patricia Everman Myers; machine-quilted by New Traditions. Hand-dyed fabrics are by Fabrics to Dye For (see Resources on page 144).

⊙ 30 Minutes ⊙

2. Cut the fabric wedges.

• Cutting is one of the most important steps in kaleidoscope quilting. If the wedges are not cut accurately, the completed blocks will not be smooth and flat.

• Use a Kaleidoscope Wedge Ruler to cut accurate pieces.

Note from Nancy: See our Resources on page 144 to order this special ruler.

  – Position the tip of the ruler at the upper edge of the pieced section.
  – Align the horizontal markings on the ruler with the seams on the pieced section.
  – Cut along both sides of the ruler *(Diagram F)*.
  – Flip the ruler top to bottom. The tip of the ruler now lies at the opposite edge of the pieced section. Cut another fabric wedge *(Diagram G)*.

• Cut eight wedges for each kaleidoscope unit (32 total).

Note from Nancy: Take your time as you cut these wedges. I generally spend more time cutting than sewing when I make kaleidoscope projects. The edges are cut on the bias and, therefore, can stretch. Before cutting each wedge, check that the ruler's markings are parallel to the seams of the pieced section. If the fabric seams do not align with the ruler markings after the ruler is flipped, realign the ruler and make a clean cut at the edge to reestablish perfectly shaped wedges.

• Stack two piles of wedges, one with the light at the widest end of the wedge and the other with the dark at the widest end *(Diagram H)*.

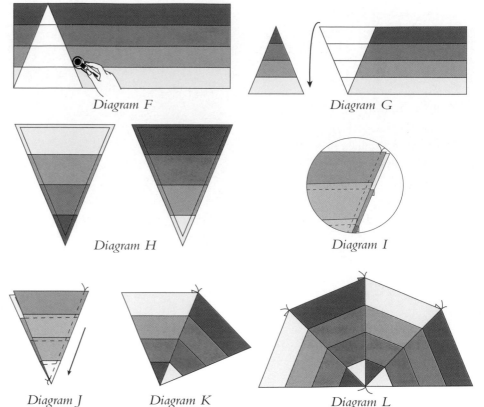

Diagram F

Diagram G

Diagram H

Diagram I

Diagram J

Diagram K

Diagram L

⊙ 30 Minutes ⊙

3. Stitch the light and dark wedges into pairs.

• Place the light wedge on the bottom and the dark wedge on top, with the right sides together.

• Make sure that all the seams align.
  – The seam allowances will be pressed **up** on one wedge section and **down** on the other *(Diagram I)*.
  – Roll the edges between your fingers until the two seams align perfectly.
  – Pin the seam intersections or finger-pin as you stitch. Remember that these edges are cut on the bias and will stretch. This can work to your advantage as you try to align seam intersections.

• Stitch from the widest end to the point of the wedges *(Diagram J)*.

• Press the seam allowances in one direction *(Diagram K)*.

• Join four pairs of wedges in the same manner.

4. Stitch the pairs together to form two half blocks *(Diagram L)*.

• Join a light wedge to a dark wedge.

• Press the seams in the same direction as those joining the wedges into pairs.

• Join the remaining pairs into a half block, following the same procedure.

5. Stitch the half blocks together to create full blocks.

• Pin the blocks at the center intersection to assure that the point is perfectly matched. Because eight wedges are joined at the center, this area is very bulky.

• Stitch slowly so that the blocks remain precisely matched at the center.

⊙ 10 Minutes ⊙

6. Cut two 5¼" (13.125 cm) squares from both the medium/dark and very dark fabrics for the kaleidoscope blocks. Cut each square in half diagonally to make corner triangles.

☺ 10 Minutes ☺

7. Stitch a triangle to each corner of the block.

• Meet a corner triangle to the corner of the block, with the right sides together.

• Aim the point of the triangle toward the center of the kaleidoscope block *(Diagram M)*.

• Stitch, using a ¼" (0.6 cm) seam allowance. Press the seam allowance toward the triangle.

Note from Nancy: Check that the blocks are perfectly square after the corners are attached. Position each completed block on a rotary cutting mat; check that the horizontal and vertical edges are parallel to the horizontal and vertical markings on the mat. If the edges are uneven, use a ruler and a rotary cutter to square the block.

QUILT ASSEMBLY
☺ 20 Minutes ☺

1. Position a light block next to a dark one.

2. Stitch the blocks together, alternating a dark block next to a light one *(Diagram N)*.

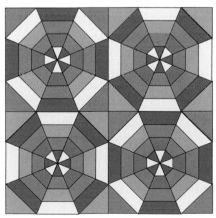

Diagram N

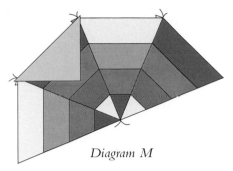

Diagram M

☺ 20 Minutes ☺

3. Add borders to the quilt.

• Add two 1½" x 30½" (3.8 cm x 77.3 cm) inner side borders.

• Add two 1½" x 32½" (3.8 cm x 82.8 cm) inner top and bottom borders.

• Add two 2½" x 32½" (6.3 cm x 82.8 cm) middle side borders.

• Add two 2½" x 36½" (6.3 cm x 92.8 cm) middle top and bottom borders.

• Add two 3½" x 36½" (9 cm x 92.8 cm) outer side borders.

• Add two 3½" x 42½" (9 cm x 108.3 cm) outer top and bottom borders.

QUILTING & FINISHING

1. Layer the backing (facedown), the batting, and the quilt top (faceup). Baste the layers together.

2. Quilt as desired. The quilt shown was machine-quilted in an allover oak leaf design.

3. Join 2¼"-wide (5.6 cm-wide) strips into one continous piece to make binding. Add the binding to the quilt.

Four-Patch Quilt

LEARN A NEW TECHNIQUE FOR CREATING FOUR-PATCH UNITS. I'LL SHOW YOU
AN EASY STRIP-PIECING METHOD TO SPEED THE SEWING WITHOUT EVER
HAVING TO CUT SQUARE SHAPES FOR THE ALTERNATE BLOCKS.

Finished Size: 44½" x 44½"
(113.3 cm x 113.3 cm)
Blocks: 8"-square (20.5 cm-square)
Four-Patch Units

MATERIALS

1 yard (0.95 m) Fabric A for blocks
and binding
1 yard (0.95 m) Fabric B for blocks
and border
1 yard (0.95 m) Fabric C for blocks
1¼ yards (1.15 m) fabric for backing
1¼ yards (1.15 m) batting

CUTTING
⏲ 10 Minutes ⏲

Measurements include ¼" (0.6 cm)
seam allowances.

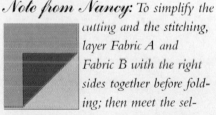

Note from Nancy: To simplify the
cutting and the stitching,
layer Fabric A and
Fabric B with the right
sides together before folding; then meet the sel-
vages. Fold and cut as detailed above.
After cutting the strips, don't separate the
colors. They are ready to be stitched
together to make the Four-Patch.

From Fabric A, cut:
- Six 2½" x 44" (6.3 cm x 112 cm)
  strips for blocks.
- Five 2¼" x 44" (5.6 cm x 112 cm)
  strips for binding.

From Fabric B, cut:
- Six 2½" x 44" (6.3 cm x 112 cm)
  strips for blocks.
- Four 2½" x 44" (6.3 cm x 112 cm)
  strips for borders.

From Fabric C, cut:
- Six 4½" x 44" (11.5 cm x 112 cm)
  strips for blocks.

BLOCK ASSEMBLY
⏲ 30 Minutes ⏲

1. Stitch the strips together, creating
a strip set.
- Join the lengthwise edges of Fabric
A and Fabric B, with the right sides
together *(Diagram A)*.
- At the end of the seam, do not raise
the presser foot or cut the threads.
Butt the second set of strips to the
first and continue sewing, chain-
piecing the strips together *(Diagram B)*.
- Continue to join all six strip sets.
Then clip the threads between the
strips to separate them.
- Divide the strip sets into two stacks
of three strips each, which are mirror
images of each other. One strip set
will have Fabric A on the left, and
the other will have Fabric B on the
left *(Diagram C)*.
- Join Fabric C to each strip set,
using the stitching techniques
detailed above.
- Separate the strip sets into two
stacks, with like strip sets together.
One will be A/B/C and the other
B/A/C *(Diagram D)*.
- Press the seams flat. Then press the
seams in one stack toward Fabric C and
the seams in the other stack toward
Fabric B *(Diagram E)*. This distributes
the bulk and makes it easier to match
intersections when joining the blocks.

$\longrightarrow$

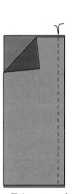
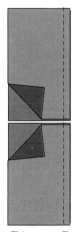

Diagram A   *Diagram B*

Diagram C

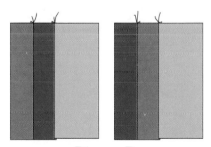

Diagram D

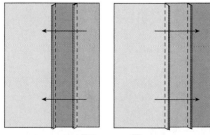

Diagram E

2. Crosscut the strip sets.
• Stack the strip sets from each grouping, with the right sides together, stacking Fabric C and aligning the straight edges and the seams as perfectly as possible *(Diagram F)*.
• Crosscut the strip sets into 2½" (6.3 cm) sections, using rotary cutting techniques *(Diagram G)*. Keep the cross cuts in pairs.
3. Join pairs to create a set, with the right sides together, using chain-piecing to create a Four-Patch with an attached block. This creates a set *(Diagram H)*. Press the seams flat and then to one side.

QUILT ASSEMBLY
⏱ 30 Minutes ⏱

1. Create the quilt top.
• Divide the Four-Patch sections into two groups, one with Fabric C block on top and the other with the Four-Patch on top.
• Chain-piece the sections together. Press as detailed above. Cut the blocks apart *(Diagram I)*.
2. Lay out the 25 blocks, five across and five down. Sew each row together and then join the rows to complete the quilt top *(Diagram J)*.
3. Measure the length of the quilt. Trim two border strips to this measurement and add them to opposite sides of the quilt.
4. Measure the width of the quilt, including the borders. Trim two border strips to this measurement and add them to the quilt top and bottom *(Diagram K)*.

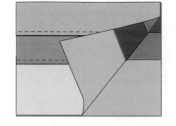

Diagram F

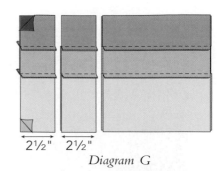
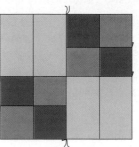

2½" 2½"

Diagram G

Diagram H

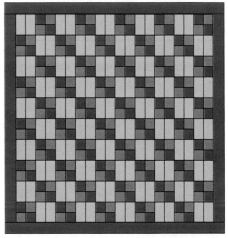

Diagram I

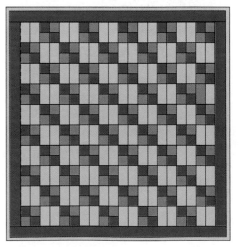

Diagram J

Diagram K

QUILTING & FINISHING
1. Layer the backing (facedown), the batting, and the quilt top (faceup). Baste the layers together.
2. Quilt as desired. The quilt shown was quilted in-the-ditch.
3. Join 2¼"-wide (5.6 cm-wide) strips into one continous piece to make binding. Add the binding to the quilt *(Diagram L)*.

Diagram L

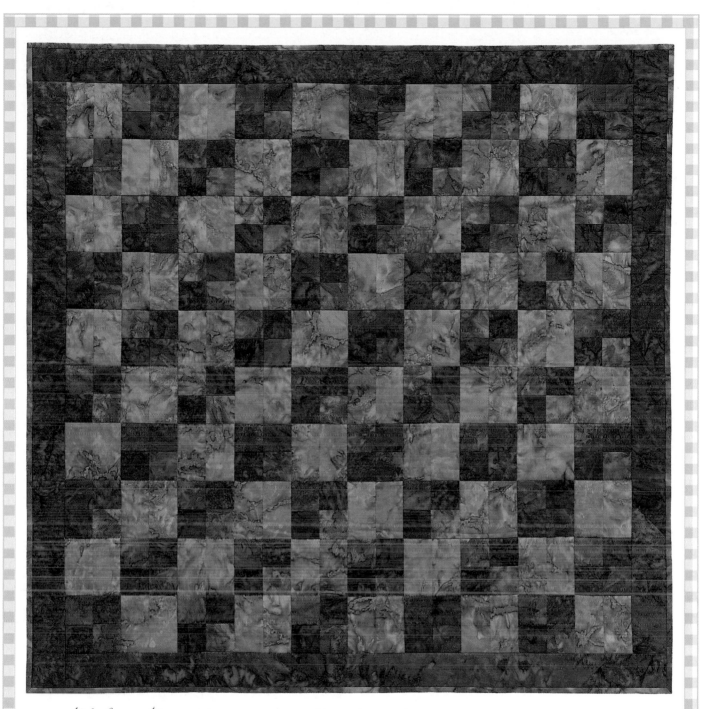

Note from Nancy: This Four-Patch assembly is a favorite of mine. I like the idea of working with neat strip sets instead of keeping up with lots of small squares. The blue marble print that I used in this quilt minimizes the split setting pieces. You might also consider doing some fancy machine quilting in these open areas. Avoid using novelty prints or directional prints, as they will be split in the middle.

Trip Around the World Pillow

FOR YEARS, QUILTERS HAVE STITCHED THE POPULAR TRIP AROUND THE WORLD PATTERN. THE KEY TO CREATING THIS DESIGN IS TO SEW SIX NARROW FABRIC STRIPS INTO A TUBE AND THEN CUT SMALLER SECTIONS. IT'S A SIMPLIFIED APPROACH TO PATCHWORK.

Pillow designed by
Nancy Zieman

Finished Size: 19" x 19"
(48 cm x 48 cm)

MATERIALS

Choose six fabrics:

• Begin with an interesting multi-colored print fabric.

• Choose five solid fabrics included in or complementing the print fabric. Fabrics should include color values ranging from dark to light.

• Purchase the following yardages to make the pillow:

  • ⅛ yard (0.15 m) print fabric
  • ⅛ yard (0.15 m) each of four solid fabrics
  • ¾ yard (0.70 m) of one solid light fabric for blocks, border, and pillow backing

CUTTING
🕐 30 Minutes 🕐

From the print fabric, cut:
- Two 1½"-wide (3.8 cm-wide) strips. One is for the Trip Around the World strip set and the other is for the Nine-Patch corner blocks.

From each solid fabric, cut:
- One 1½"-wide (3.8 cm-wide) strip for the Trip Around the World strip set.

From the solid light fabric, cut:
- Two 1½"-wide (3.8 cm-wide) strips. One is for the Trip Around the World strip set and the other is for the Nine-Patch corner blocks.
- One 20" (51 cm) square for the pillow backing.
- Four 3½" x 13½" (9 cm x 34.3 cm) strips for the borders.

ASSEMBLY
🕐 30 Minutes 🕐

Measurements include ¼" (0.6 cm) seam allowances.

1. Stitch the fabrics into a six-strip strip set.
- Arrange the six strips from darkest to lightest, starting with the print. Number the strips and tape them to a bulletin board to serve as a reference *(Diagram A)*.
- Stitch the strips together in numerical order, forming a strip set *(Diagram B)*. Press the seams open.

🕐 30 Minutes 🕐

2. Cut the strip set into sections.
- Cut the sections for Row A.
  - Cut eight 1½" (3.8 cm) sections, cutting across the strip set. Stack the sections with the leaf print on top. Label this group Section A *(Diagram C)*.
  - Stitch the remainder of the strip set into a tube, using a ¼" (0.6 cm) seam allowance and meeting the lengthwise edge of Color 1 to the lengthwise edge of Color 6 *(Diagram D)*.
- Cut the sections for Row B.
  - Cut four 1½" (3.8 cm) sections from the tube.
  - Remove the stitching between Colors 1 and 2. Instead of the print fabric, the darkest solid fabric is on top.
  - Stack the sections and label this group Row B *(Diagram E)*.
- Cut sections for Row C.
  - Cut four 1½" (3.8 cm) sections from the tube.
  - Remove the stitching between Colors 2 and 3.
  - Stack the sections and label this group Row C.
- Repeat the process for sections D, E, and F, counting down one additional seam for each grouping.

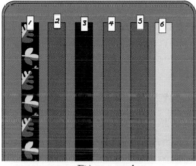

Diagram A

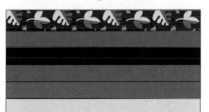

Diagram B

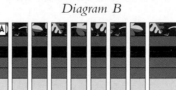

Diagram C

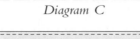

Diagram D

🕐 30 Minutes 🕐

3. Arrange the quilt rows into the Trip Around the World design.
- Place Rows A through F next to each other, starting with Row A at the left and ending with Row F at the right *(Diagram F)*.

> *Note from Nancy:* Small sections like those for this pillow can easily get misplaced or out of sequence. Arrange the rows on a terry towel to help organize them, to make it easy to move them to the machine for stitching, and/or to store them.

- Set up the sewing machine.
  - Set the stitch length to 12 stitches per inch or less (2.5).
  - Thread the machine with all-purpose thread.
  - Replace the conventional presser foot with the Little Foot®.
- Stitch the rows together *(Diagram G)*.
  - Chain-piece Rows A and B together, sewing four sets of the rows.
  - Chain-piece Rows C and D together; sew four sets.
  - Chain-piece Rows E and F together; sew four sets. ⟶

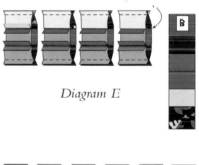

Diagram E

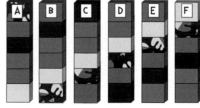

Diagram F

Diagram G

- Use a stiletto to keep the seam allowances in place during stitching *(Diagram H)*. Seam lines should be aligned.

• Press the seams open *(Diagram I)*. Cut the stitching between the chained pairs.

• Stitch the pairs (A/B, C/D, and E/F) together to form four squares as shown in *Diagram J*. (Four of Row A remain.)

• Place the four squares on a tabletop to form a larger square, with Color 1 (the print fabric) in each of the inside corners. Slightly separate the squares *(Diagram K)*.

• Place a strip of Row A between each square *(Diagram L)*.

• Cut a 1½" (3.8 cm) square from Color 5. Place that square in the center of the design *(Diagram M)*.

4. Stitch all the sections together, using a ¼" (0.6 cm) seam allowance.

☺ 20 Minutes ☺

5. Add borders to create a pillow top.

• Stitch two 3½" x 13½" (9 cm x 34.3 cm) border strips to opposite sides of the patchwork design *(Diagram N)*.

• Using 1½" (3.8 cm) strips from the print and the light solid, cut twenty 1½" (3.8 cm) print squares and sixteen 1½" (3.8 cm) light solid squares. Referring to *Diagram O,* join the squares to make four Nine-Patch blocks.

   - Stitch a Nine-Patch block to each end of the two remaining borders *(Diagram O)*.

   - Stitch the borders to the patchwork design *(Diagram P)*.

6. Attach a backing to the pillow top, following your favorite technique. Stuff the pillow with polyester fiberfill or insert a pillow form.

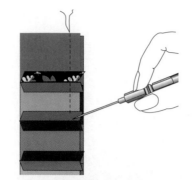

Diagram H

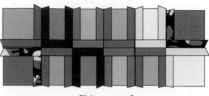

Diagram I

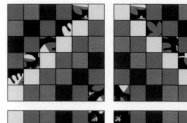

Diagram K

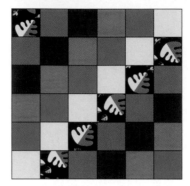

Diagram J

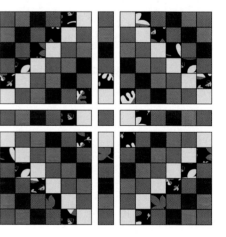

Diagram M

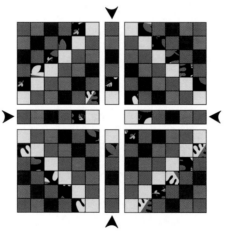

Diagram L

Diagram O

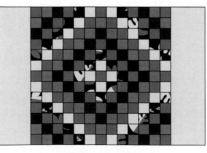

Diagram N

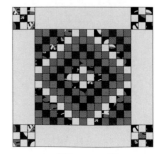

Diagram P

Caring For and Cleaning Quilts

TO KEEP A QUILT IN PRISTINE CONDITION WOULD MEAN STORING IT IN IDEAL ARCHIVAL CONDITIONS AND NEVER USING IT. BUT WE MAKE QUILTS TO USE AND TO ENJOY! SO, TRY THESE TIPS AT HOME.

SAFEKEEPING

• If you display a quilt, it is bound to fade over time. But you can minimize the fading by keeping the quilt out of strong sunlight and storing it properly when not in use.

• Rotate the quilt you display with other quilts every few months to reduce exposure. Consider making seasonal quilts in the same size to rotate as the seasons change.

• Store an unused quilt—with as few folds as possible—in a cotton pillowcase.

• Don't store quilts in plastic bags, which trap moisture.

• To discourage creases in stored quilts, tuck acid-free paper inside the folds.

CLEANING

• Do not wash your quilts often.

• Spot-clean whenever possible.

• Remember that, often, a good airing can freshen a quilt.

• Never dry-clean a quilt. It can leave harmful chemicals in the fibers and cause damage to your quilt over time.

• When you must wash a quilt, use a mild soap, such as Ensure or Orvis Paste (a shampoo originally designed for livestock).

• Wash large quilts by hand in the bathtub. Fill the tub with lukewarm water, adding the amount of soap specified on the label. Immerse the quilt and gently agitate it with your hands to disperse the soap. Let the quilt soak for 10 to 15 minutes; then drain the tub.

• Do not wring the quilt dry. Drain the tub and press out the excess water from the quilt.

• Rinse until the water runs clear.

• You can machine-dry your quilt on a cool or air setting to smooth out wrinkles and to fluff it a bit.

3

Fleece Quilts

Traditionally, quilts are made with three layers: the quilt top, the batting, and the backing. In contrast, fleece quilts require only one or two layers. THE HIGH-LOFT FLEECE SERVES AS BOTH THE BATTING AND THE BACKING to create a comfy blanket or throw. Best of all, because the edges won't ravel, you're finished with the quilt once you've sewn the pieces together! You can use the zigzag feature on your sewing machine or a serger to join the pieces. YOU'LL BE PLEASED AT HOW THIS OUTERWEAR FABRIC DOUBLES AS A PERFECT QUILTING FABRIC.

Guidelines for Fleece Quilts

HIGH-LOFT FLEECES—SUCH AS POLARFLEECE®, POLARTEC®, NORDIC™ FLEECE, ESKIMO FLEECE, AND ARCTIC® FLEECE—ARE FAVORITE FABRICS FOR CASUAL PULLOVERS, VESTS, AND JACKETS. ALTHOUGH SOME PEOPLE DESCRIBE ANY HIGH-LOFT FLEECE AS POLARFLEECE AND USE IT AS A GENERIC TERM, THE NAME IS A REGISTERED TRADEMARK; THE SAME IS TRUE OF POLARTEC. THOSE TERMS CAN BE USED APPROPRIATELY ONLY FOR FLEECES PRODUCED BY MALDEN MILLS.

FABRIC FACTS

High-loft fleeces have some common characteristics:

- Provide warmth without weight.
- Are relatively lightweight.
- Are reversible.
- Don't ravel.

With these characteristics, high-loft fleeces are perfect candidates for blankets, throws, and quilts. Using super-sized blocks or strips of fleece, you can sew or serge quick quilts, blankets, or throws in a few hours. The result is sensational-looking patchwork with texture and loft. High-loft fleeces are usually 100% polyester and are 60" (152.5 cm) wide. The extra width is an added benefit when creating over-size quilt blocks.

Note from Nancy: There are many varieties of fleece, including blends (poly-ester/Lycra™) intended for active sportswear; heavyweight fleeces (Polartec® 300) intended for outerwear; and lightweight fleeces (Polartec® 100) intended for warmer climates. These specialty fleeces are not recommended for quilting or patchwork. Use a medium-weight fleece, such as Polartec® 200, for your quilting-related projects.

STRIP-CUTTING TECHNIQUES

Use these guidelines when creating a fleece quilt.

- Work on a cutting mat. Fold the fleece and meet the selvages. Fold it in half again, placing the wrong sides together and meeting the first fold to the selvages. To determine the right side of the fabric, pull the fabric on the crosswise grain. The fabric rolls to the wrong side *(Diagram A)*.
- Place a 6" x 24" (15 cm x 61 cm) ruler near the right edge of the fold-ed fabric, with a small amount of fabric extending beyond the ruler. Trim the fabric edge, using a 60 mm rotary cutter *(Diagram B)*.

Diagram A

Note from Nancy: Since fleece is very lofty, it helps to use a 60 mm cutter, which has a large blade, to cut through multiple layers. For added leverage when cutting through several layers, hold the cutter perpendicular to the ruler and hold the ruler securely to prevent it from slipping.

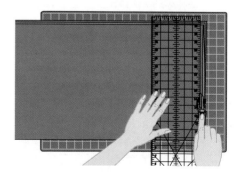

Diagram B

- Turn the fabric or mat so that the previous right edge is now the left edge.
- Align the ruler along the cut edge and cut the strips *(Diagram C)*.

SEAMING OPTIONS

Sewing machine:

- Set the machine for a straight stitch, 8 to 10 stitches (3.5 to 4.0) per inch.
- Attach a ¼"-wide (0.6 cm-wide) quilting foot or adjust the needle position to achieve a ¼" (0.6 cm) seam allowance.
- With the right sides together, stitch a ¼" (0.6 cm) seam allowance, using the presser foot as a guide.
- Change the settings on the machine to a zigzag with a wide stitch width and a long stitch length
- Zigzag the seam edges together.
- Test the stitching on a scrap of fleece. If the seam buckles, lengthen the stitch.
- Finger-press the seam allowances to one side *(Diagram D)*.

Serger:

- Use all-purpose serger thread.
- Set the serger for a 4-thread overlock stitch. Refer to your owner's manual for specific settings.
- With the right sides together, serge with a ¼" (0.6 cm) seam allowance *(Diagram E)*.
- Test serging on a scrap of fleece. If the seam buckles, lengthen the stitch.
- Finger-press the seam allowances to one side.

FINGER PRESSING

An iron and high-loft fleeces are not compatible, as ironing will flatten the nap of the fabric. Yet pressing is needed. After seaming, finger-press the seam, using your fingers to pat the seam in one direction.

If finger pressing is not enough, **gently steam the fabric with an iron without touching the iron surface to the fabric** and pat the fabric with your hand. Let the fabric dry on a flat surface.

Note from Nancy: If your serger has a differential feed setting that controls the "bite" of the feed dogs, test the setting at different levels. An adjustment can easily prevent the seam from stretching.

Serging Fleece Quilts

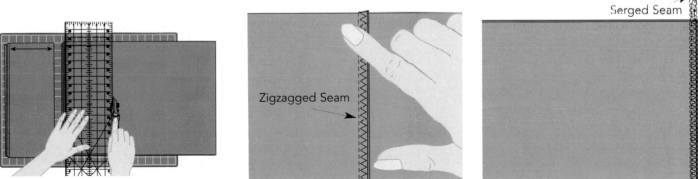

Diagram C

Zigzagged Seam

Diagram D

Serged Seam

Diagram E

Checkerboard Fleece

START YOUR ADVENTURE OF USING HIGH-LOFT FLEECES AS QUILTING FABRICS
BY CREATING A CHECKERBOARD QUILT. THIS EASY YET DRAMATIC-LOOKING BEDCOVER
CAN BE SEWN OR SERGED, BUT SERGING IS THE FASTEST OPTION.

Quilt by
Nancy Zieman

Finished Size: 67½" x 94½"
(171.8 cm x 240.3 cm)

Blocks: Eight 13½" (34.3 cm)
Nine-Patch Blocks

MATERIALS

2½ yards (2.30 m) red fleece
2¼ yards (2.10 m) black fleece

CUTTING
🕐 30 Minutes 🕐

Refer to the fleece cutting and
sewing instructions on pages 40 and
41. Measurements include ¼" (0.6
cm) seam allowances. Polarfleece®
is 60" (152.5 cm) wide.

From the red fleece, cut:

- Five 5"-wide (12.5 cm-wide) strips
  for blocks.
- Four 14"-wide (35.5 cm-wide)
  strips. Cut strips into two 14" x 41"
  (35.5 cm x 104 cm) top and bottom
  borders and four 14" x 27½" (35.5
  cm x 69.8 cm) side borders.

From the black fleece, cut:

- Four 5"-wide (12.5 cm-wide)
  strips for blocks.
- Four 14"-wide (35.5 cm-wide)
  strips. Cut strips into 13 (14" or
  35.5 cm) setting blocks.

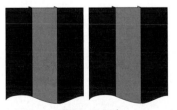

Diagram A

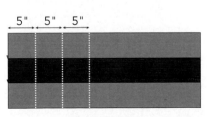

Diagram B

BLOCK ASSEMBLY
🕐 30 Minutes 🕐

Note from Nancy: Use a serger
for the fastest construction. Test scraps
of your fabrics before sewing your quilt
pieces. You may find that adjusting the
serger's differential feed will keep the
fleece fabrics feeding evenly as you
serge them together. Please
refer to the general fleece
instructions for sewing
and serging specifics.

1. Join one red strip to each side of
one black strip to make one red strip
set. Make two red strip sets *(Diagram
A)*. Cut the strip sets into 16 (5"-
wide or 12.5 cm-wide) segments
(Diagram B).
2. Join one black strip to each side
of one red strip to make one black
strip set. Cut the strip set into eight
5"-wide (12.5 cm-wide) segments.
3. Join two red segments and one
black segment to make one Nine-
Patch block *(Diagram C)*.
4. Make eight Nine-Patch blocks.

ROW ASSEMBLY
🕐 30 Minutes 🕐

1. Create one row by stitching or
serging two Nine-Patch blocks to
opposite sides of a solid black block,
with the right sides together. Make
two more for a total of three rows.
2. Create another large row by
sewing two solid black blocks to
opposite sides of a Nine-Patch block,

Diagram C

with the right sides together. Make
two rows.
3. Stitch or serge together by alternating rows as shown in *Diagram D*.

QUILT ASSEMBLY
🕐 30 Minutes 🕐

1. Stitch or serge a black square
between two red rectangles. Repeat
to make two side borders.
2. Stitch or serge two solid black
blocks to each end of a red rectangle.
Repeat to make the top and bottom
borders.
3. Stitch or serge the side borders
to the long sides of the center panel,
matching the solid black block with
its neighboring Nine-Patch block.
4. Stitch or serge the top and the
bottom borders to the center panel,
matching the black corner blocks to
the ends of the side borders.

FINISHING

1. Fold under and pin a ⅝" (1.5 cm)
hem along all the edges.
2. Straightstitch ½" (1.3 cm) from
the fold.

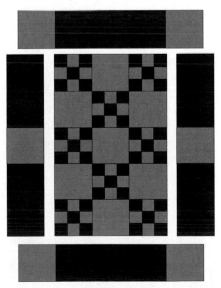

Diagram D

Plainly Amish Fleece Quilt

YOU CAN ALMOST HEAR THE CLIP-CLOP OF A HORSE-DRAWN CARRIAGE IN THE DISTANCE AS YOU SERGE OR SEW THIS EASY THROW. IT FEATURES A CHARACTERISTIC AMISH DESIGN IN A COMPLETELY UNCHARACTERISTIC FABRIC: FLEECE. ENJOY THE PROCESS OF CREATING, AS WELL AS USING, THIS COZY QUILT.

**Quilt by
Nancy
Zieman**

Finished Size: 68" x 68"
(173 cm x 173 cm)

MATERIALS

1 yard (0.95 m) navy fleece
1¼ yards (1.15 m) green fleece
1¼ yards (1.15 m) red fleece
8 yards (7.35 m) stretch binding
(1⅝"-wide [4 cm-wide] stretching
binding is 89% nylon and 11%
Lycra™.)

CUTTING
🕐 30 Minutes 🕐

Please refer to the fleece cutting and
sewing instructions on pages 40 and
41 and to *Fleece Cutting Diagram*
below. Measurements include ¼" (0.6
cm) seam allowances.

From the navy fleece, cut:
• One 30" (76 cm) center square.
• Four 6" (15 cm) center sashing
  squares.

From the green fleece, cut:
• Four 6"-wide (15 cm-wide) strips.
  Cut strips into four 6" x 57¾"
  (15 cm x 147 cm) strips for outer
  borders.
• Two 6"-wide (15 cm-wide) strips.
  Cut strips into four 6" x 30" (15
  cm x 76 cm) center sashing strips.

From the red fleece, cut:
• Two 29½" (74.8 cm) squares. Cut
  squares in half diagonally to make
  four corner setting triangles.
• Four 6" (15 cm) squares for outer
  sashing squares.

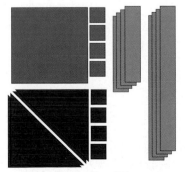

Fleece Cutting Diagram

BLOCK ASSEMBLY
🕐 30 Minutes 🕐

1. Join one green center sashing
strip to the top and the bottom of
the navy center square *(Diagram A)*.
2. Join one navy 6" (15 cm) square
to each end of the remaining green
center sashing strips *(Diagram B)*. Add
the strips to the sides of the navy
center square *(Diagram C)*.

Note from Nancy: When seams
intersect, finger-press the meeting seams
in opposite directions to stagger the
bulk of the seams.

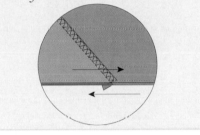

3. Join one red setting triangle to
each side of the navy center unit
(Diagram D).
4. Join one green border strip to
opposite sides of the center unit.

Note from Nancy: Stitch or serge
with the main block facing up to ensure
that the seam allowances at the triangle
point are sewn down in opposite directions. Staggering the seam allowances
will prevent dimples in the seam.

5. Add a red 6" (15 cm) square to
each end of the remaining green
border strips. Add the borders to the
top and the bottom of the quilt
(Diagram E). ⟶

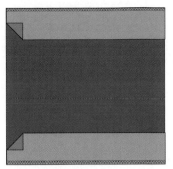

Diagram A

Diagram B

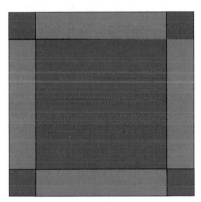

Diagram C

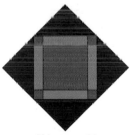

Diagram D

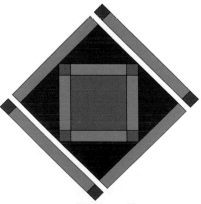

Diagram E

FINISHING

Note from Nancy: *Stretch binding is not a traditional binding for most quilts, yet it is a common fleece finish used by sewing enthusiasts. The binding has two-way stretch and is a blend of nylon and Lycra™. It generally is sold for $1 per yard and is a neat way to finish this nontraditional quilt.*

1. Fold under ¼" (0.6 cm) at one end of the binding.

2. Mark the quilt top ½" (1.3 cm) from each corner. On the right side of the quilt, in the center of one side, position the binding, aligning the edges of the binding and the fleece. Start stitching here.

3. Stitch the binding to the quilt top, using a straight stitch and the presser foot as a seam guide. Stop stitching at the marked point. Lock the stitches *(Diagram F)*.

4. Fold the binding at a 45° angle, aligning the cut edges of the binding with the cut edge of the fleece *(Diagram G)*.

5. Fold the binding down, meeting the binding fold to the top edge of the quilt and the binding edges to the quilt side edge. Stitch a ½" (1.3 cm) seam on the side, starting at the fold *(Diagram H)*.

6. Repeat at the remaining corners. Overlap the binding at the starting point and trim the excess binding.

7. Fold the binding to the wrong side, covering the stitching; tuck in the corners to form miters. Pin.

8. Stitch in-the-ditch on the right side of the quilt, sewing in the well of the seam through both layers to secure the binding *(Diagram I)*.

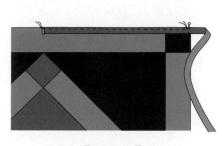

Diagram F

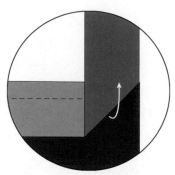

Diagram G

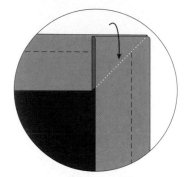

Diagram H

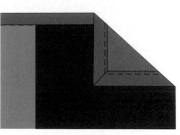

Diagram I

Serged Log Cabin Throw

SERGE OR SEW A SUPER-SIZED LOG CABIN THROW IN TWO EVENINGS. THIS INCREDIBLY SOFT THROW IS THE PERFECT SIZE FOR SNUGGLING IN FRONT OF THE TV OR KEEPING WARM AT A FOOTBALL GAME. IT IS MADE FROM A SINGLE LAYER OF HIGH-LOFT FLEECE, ONE OF THE EASIEST FABRICS TO SEW.

Throw by
Donna Fenske

Finished Size: 55" x 55"
(139.5 cm x 139.5 cm)
Blocks: Four 27½" (69.8 cm) Log
Cabin Blocks

MATERIALS

¼ yard (0.25 m) or one 6" x 24"
(15 cm x 61 cm) strip red fleece
¾ yard (0.70 m) green fleece
1¼ yards (1.15 m) navy fleece

CUTTING
🕐 30 Minutes 🕐

Please refer to the fleece cutting and sewing instructions on pages 40 and 41. Measurements include ¼" (0.6 cm) seam allowances. Polarfleece® is 60" (152.5 cm) wide.

From the red fleece, cut:
• Four 6" (15 cm) squares.

From the green fleece, cut:
• Four 6"-wide (15 cm–wide) strips.

From the navy fleece, cut:
• Six 6"-wide (15 cm–wide) strips.

→

MACHINE SETUP
⏱ 10 Minutes ⏱

For serger seaming:

Adjust the serger for a flatlock stitch, threading the machine with all-purpose serger thread that matches one of the predominant fleece colors. Test the stitching; if the seam buckles, try lengthening the stitch and loosening the needle tension. Check your owner's manual for specific recommendations for your machine.

Note from Nancy: The flatlock stitch, as the name implies, can be flattened after serging, eliminating the bulk of the seam. If you've never used a flatlock stitch before, this is the perfect time to start, since fleece is a forgiving fabric. As an option, you could use a traditional overlock stitch instead of the flatlock stitch, as detailed on page 41. Test a sample of both stitches on a swatch to see which option you prefer.

For traditional seaming:

Refer to the fleece cutting and sewing instructions on pages 40 and 41.

BLOCK ASSEMBLY
⏱ 30 Minutes ⏱

1. Lay one red square on top of one green strip, with the right sides together. Serge the edge *(Diagram A)*.
2. Place a second red square at least 1" (2.5 cm) from the end of the first square. Stitch or serge *(Diagram B)*. Repeat with all four blocks.

Note from Nancy: Attention serging enthusiasts! As each new block is added, the presser foot tends to push the top block, causing corners to misalign. As you approach a new block, raise the presser foot with your finger. Flatten the top block, lower the foot, and continue serging.

• If using the flatlock stitch, after attaching all four blocks, open the seam and flatten the stitch, gently applying tension on each side of the seam *(Diagram C)*.
3. Cut 6" (15 cm) segments from the sewn strip *(Diagram D)*, placing the ruler over the flattened blocks. (The fabric may stretch slightly during stitching, so it may be necessary to square the segments.)
4. Add the third strip.
• Rotate the segments one quarter turn to the right so that the newest strip is on top. Stack the blocks with the **wrong** side up *(Diagram E)*.
• Place another green strip with the right side up. Join the blocks to the green strip, with the right sides together, again leaving 1" (2.5 cm) spacing between the blocks. Stitch or serge the blocks together.
• Flatten the flatlock stitch, if needed.
• Cut the strips apart, aligning the 5¾" (14.5 cm) ruler marking over the serged seam *(Diagram F)*.

Diagram A

Diagram B

Diagram C

Diagram D

Diagram E

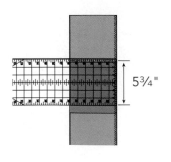

5¾"

Diagram F

• Open each seam and flatten the stitching. Stack the blocks with the newest color on top and the wrong sides up.

• Repeat, using the same technique to add two navy strips, followed by two green strips and two more navy strips *(Diagram G)*.

5. Join four blocks in this manner.

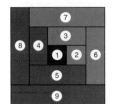

Numbers indicate piecing order.

Diagram G

QUILT ASSEMBLY
⊙ 20 Minutes ⊙

1. Arrange the blocks as shown in the photo and in *Diagram H.*

2. Stitch or serge the four blocks together.

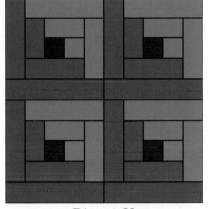

Diagram H

FINISHING

To finish the throw, fold under ½" (1.3 cm) on the outer edges and straightstitch or zigzag the hem in place *(Diagram I)*.

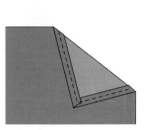

Diagram I

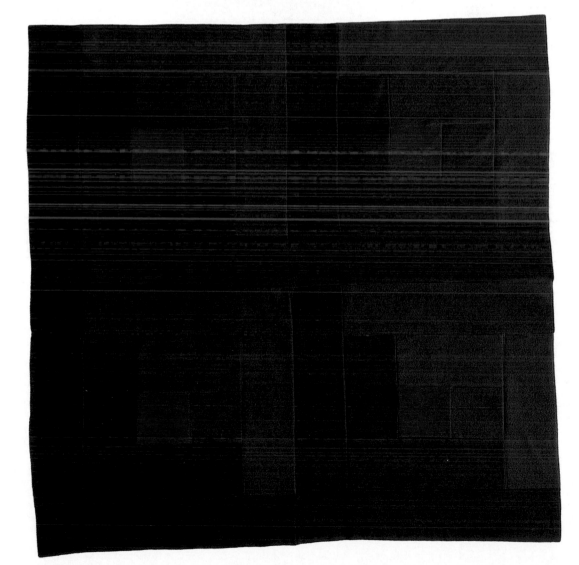

Fleece-and-Flannel Throw

IN THIS QUILT, HIGH-LOFT FLEECE SERVES AS BOTH THE BATTING AND THE BACKING TO CREATE A COMFY BLANKET.

MATERIALS

1¾ yards (1.60 m) flannel for quilt top
2 yards (1.85 m) high-loft fleece for
   backing

CUTTING
⏱ 20 Minutes ⏱

1. Smooth the flannel piece on top of
the fleece, with the wrong sides facing.
2. Cut the fleece 3" to 4" (7.5 cm to
10 cm) longer and wider than the quilt
top. (This provides 1½" to 2" [3.8 cm
to 5 cm] quilt borders around all the
sides of the quilt top. Adjust the borders as desired *[Diagram A].*)

Diagram A

*Note from Nancy: Polarfleece™
is 60" (152.5 cm) wide, compared to
most quilt fabrics, which are only 45"
(115 cm). You'll have scraps remaining
after trimming the fleece to the desired
size. Save those scraps and use them
for other sewing or crafting projects.*

Quilt by
Nancy Zieman

QUILT ASSEMBLY
⏱ 30 Minutes ⏱

1. Layer the quilt top and the fleece, with the wrong sides together. If necessary, trim the fleece so that the borders are a uniform width.

• Baste the two layers together.

• Determine the quilting lines. Quilting lines should be a maximum of 4" to 6" (10 cm to 15 cm) apart for fleece quilting.

- Some fabrics may include design lines that make appropriate quilting lines.

- Mark the lines with chalk or with a fabric marking pencil.

• Roll the quilt sides to the middle and secure with quilt clips *(Diagram B)*.

2. Channel-stitch the quilt.

• Begin stitching at one edge of the center of the quilt and continue to the opposite edge.

• Stitch additional lines, alternating the stitching direction of adjacent rows to prevent the fabric from shifting *(Diagram C)*.

• Optional: Outline-stitch around some portions of the design to provide additional highlights *(Diagram D)*.

3. Finish the edges of the quilt.

• Miter the corners of the fleece.

- Diagonally fold the fleece to the right side at each corner of the quilt top *(Diagram E)*. Trim the excess folded fleece from the corner *(Diagram F)*.

- Fold the fleece borders to the right sides of the quilt top. Pin the borders in place. Or for an even easier way to secure the fleece, use binding and hem clips *(Diagram G)*.

• Stitch along the cut edges, sewing from the right side with a straight stitch or a zigzag *(Diagram H)*.

• Stitch the mitered edges to secure them *(Diagram I)*.

Diagram B

Diagram C

Diagram D

Diagram E

Diagram F

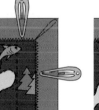

Diagram G

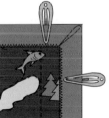

Diagram H

Diagram I

Note from Nancy: After securing the hem in place as shown in Diagram G, *you may use one of your machine's decorative stitches to sew the hem in place, as we did in this project.*

Fleece Baby Blanket

A HIGH-LOFT FLEECE BLANKET KEEPS A BABY COZY AND WARM. SIMPLE TO SEW, THE BLANKET CAN BE EMBELLISHED EASILY WITH FLEECE APPLIQUÉS AND FLEECE "YARN." MAKE AN EXTRA BLOCK TO USE AS A PILLOW.

Blanket by
Donna Fenske

Finished Size: 41½" x 41½"
(105.3 cm x 105.3 cm)

MATERIALS

½ yard (0.50 m) cream fleece
¼ yard (0.25 m) pink fleece
½ yard (0.50 m) blue fleece
½ yard (0.50 m) yellow fleece
¼ yard (0.25 m) green fleece
1¼ yards (1.15 m) stripe flannel for
backing
Pressure-sensitive fusible web
Metafil™ needle

CUTTING
⊙ 30 Minutes ⊙

Measurements include ¼" (0.6 cm)
seam allowances. Fleece is 60" (152.5
cm) wide; flannel is 45" (115 cm) wide.
Patterns are on page 55.

From the cream fleece, cut:
• One 14½"-wide (36.8 cm-wide)
strip. Cut strip into four 14½"
(36.8 cm) squares for blocks.

From the blue fleece, cut:
• Two 5"-wide (12.5 cm-wide)
strips. Cut strips into six 5" x 14½"
(12.5 cm x 36.8 cm) vertical sashing strips.

From the fleece, cut:
• Two 5"-wide (12.5 cm-wide) strips.
Cut strips into six 5" x 14½" (12.5
cm x 36.8 cm) horizontal sashing
strips.

From the green fleece, cut:
• One 6" wide (15 cm) strip. Cut strip
into nine 6" (15 cm) sashing squares.

PREPARING APPLIQUÉS
⊙ 30 Minutes ⊙

1. Trace the heart appliqués *(Diagram A)*.
• Trace 12 small hearts and two large
hearts on the paper side of the paper-
backed fusible web.
• Trace the inner stitching details.
2. Prepare and cut out the appliqués.

• Roughly cut out each appliqué
heart, leaving approximately ¼"
(0.6 cm) around the outer edges.
• Fuse the heart shapes to the wrong
side of the pink fleece, using a light
pressure on the iron to avoid flatten-
ing the nap *(Diagram B)*.

> *Note from Nancy:* This paper-
> backed fusible web is pressure sensitive
> after the paper is removed. The adhesive's
> gentle tack allows an appliqué to be posi-
> tioned without pressing. An added benefit
> is that the appliqués can be repositioned.

• Cut out each appliqué; peel off the
paper backing *(Diagram C)*. Save the
paper to use as a pattern for stitching
the details in a later step.

MACHINE SETUP
⊙ 10 Minutes ⊙

1. Insert a Metafil needle and use clear
monofilament thread in the needle.
2. Use matching thread in the bobbin.
3. Attach an appliqué or open toe foot.
4. Adjust the stitch length to 12 to 15
stitches per inch (2.0 to 2.5) setting.
(The shorter stitch length gives greater
stitching control in curved areas.)

BLOCK ASSEMBLY
⊙ 30 Minutes ⊙

1. Center one large heart on each of
two 14½" (36.8 cm) squares and fuse.
2. Arrange six small hearts in a circle
on each of the remaining squares.
Finger-press.
3. Edgestitch around each heart
appliqué *(Diagram D)*. A stabilizer is
not necessary when stitching through
two layers of fleece.
4. To stitch the inner details, overlay
the paper tracing onto each appliqué
piece. Pin in place. Stitch along the
traced lines *(Diagram E)*.
5. Tear away the paper *(Diagram E)*.

Diagram A

Diagram B

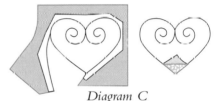

Diagram C

Diagram D

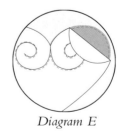

Diagram E

The needle perforates the paper,
making removal easy. ⟶

CREATING FLEECE YARN
⏱ 20 Minutes ⏱

1. Cut two ¼" (0.6 cm) or ½" (1.3 cm) cream fleece strips along the crosswise grain of the fleece. Give each strip a firm tug and the fleece becomes "fleece yarn" *(Diagram F)*.

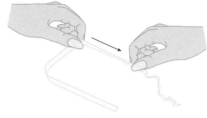

Diagram F

Note from Nancy: You may want to experiment by cutting and tugging on both the ¼" (0.6 cm) and ½" (1.3 cm) strips to see which yarn width you prefer.

2. Cut the fleece yarn into 15" (38 cm) lengths.
3. Position the fleece yarn in a simple 3"-wide (7.5 cm-wide) swirl design on each green 6" (15 cm) square.
4. Change the stitch setting to a medium zigzag stitch.
5. Zigzag over the fleece yarn

(Diagram G). After all nine 6" (15 cm) squares are complete, recut the squares into 5" (12.5 cm) squares.

QUILT ASSEMBLY
⏱ 30 Minutes ⏱

1. To create the border rows, arrange on a work surface a swirl square, a yellow 5" x 14½" (12.5 cm x 36.8 cm) strip, a swirl square, a yellow 5" x 14½" (12.5 cm x 36.8 cm) strip, and a swirl square. Meet the right sides together and stitch or serge. Finger-press the seams. Repeat to make two more strips *(Diagram H)*.
2. To create the block rows, arrange on a work surface a blue 5" x 14½" (12.5 cm x 36.8 cm) strip, a multi-heart appliqué block, a blue 5" x 14½" (12.5 cm x 36.8 cm) strip, a large heart appliqué block, and a blue 5" x 14½" strip (12.5 cm x 36.8 cm). Meet the right sides together and stitch or serge. Finger-press the seams. Repeat to make one more strip, reversing the position of the large heart and multiheart blocks.
3. On a work surface, arrange a border row, a block row, a border row, a block row, and a final border row *(Diagram I)*. Stitch or serge the rows together.

Note from Nancy: When seams intersect, finger-press the seams in opposite directions to minimize the bulk.

QUILTING & FINISHING

1. Cut the flannel into a 45" (115 cm) square.
2. Layer the backing (facedown) and the blanket top (faceup); baste.
3. Stitch in-the-ditch, stitching in the wells of the seams, to secure the blanket layer to the backing. Start in the center of the blanket and straight-stitch to the edges, following the seams of the rows and the columns *(Diagram J)*.

Diagram G

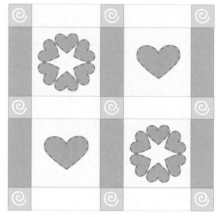

Diagram H

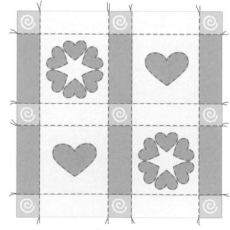

Diagram I

Diagram J

4. Hem the edges.

• Fold the corner of the flannel up over the corner of the blanket front, forming a triangle. Trim the triangle to reduce the bulk *(Diagram K)*.

• Fold the flannel so that the edges align with the edges of the blanket top *(Diagram L)*.

• Fold the flannel once more at the edge of the blanket to create the binding, mitering the corners. Pin in place.

• Straightstitch the hem in place *(Diagram M)*.

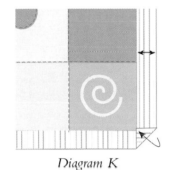

Diagram K

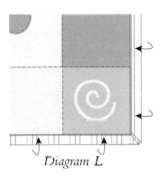

Diagram L

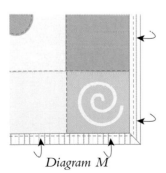

Diagram M

For the pillow shown on page 52, attach a backing to an extra block, following your favorite technique. Stuff the pillow with polyester fiberfill or insert a pillow form.

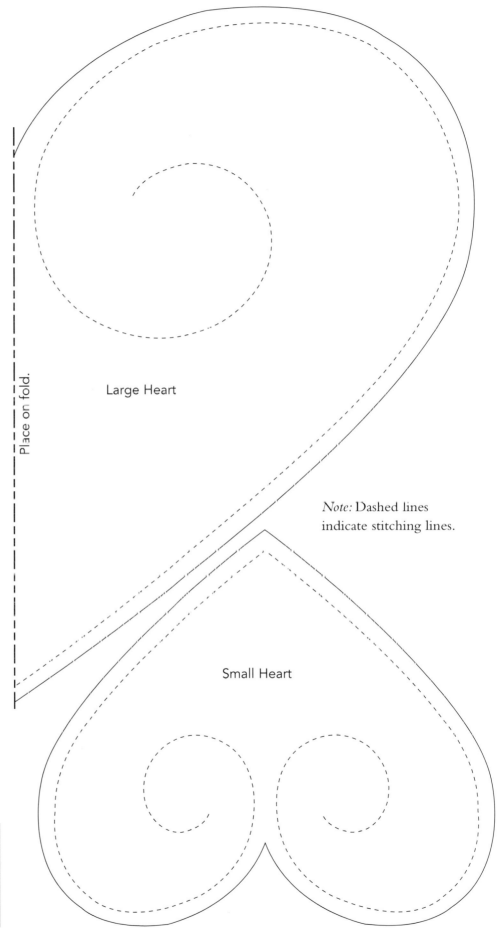

Place on fold.

Large Heart

Note: Dashed lines indicate stitching lines.

Small Heart

4

Quick Quilts from Creative Cloth

THESE DAYS, IT'S EASY TO FIND NOVELTY FABRICS WITH PRINTED PANELS OF FUN DESIGNS. You'll spot themes ranging from farming and wildlife to sports and automobiles. You've probably seen these fabrics and been reminded of someone you know—the golf print for your brother, dinosaurs for your son, or a lovely garden panel for your mom. You may have stopped short of actually buying the fabric, though, since it's often a challenge to figure out how to use large novelty panels in projects.

In the following pages, I'll give you some ideas on how to work with these panels. All of the fabrics shown are by Springs Industries. Keep in mind, however, that new designs appear every season, so you may not be able to find the exact fabrics I used. I hope that the projects will inspire you to make unique creations and will teach you some techniques that you can apply to your own quilts or to other projects.

IF YOU'RE NEW TO MACHINE QUILTING, PRINTED PANELS AFFORD YOU THE PERFECT OPPORTUNITY TO DEVELOP YOUR SKILLS. The panels are much less expensive than the yardage required to make a quilt. And because the "blocks" already exist for you, piecing a quilt top is much less time-consuming. Also, since your initial investment is minimal, you'll feel more at ease practicing machine quilting.

Apron instructions
are on page 71.

Large Printed Panels

WORKING WITH PRINTED PANELS

CHANCES ARE, YOU'LL FIND YOUR OWN EXCITING PANEL PRINTS, AND THEY'LL INSPIRE YOU TO MAKE A QUILT. USE THE GUIDELINES BELOW TO PLAN YOUR PROJECT.

1. Determine the desired size of your center panel or the center of your quilt top. Use a single panel or a composite of several different scenes. If you need setting strips for a composite panel, decide which fabrics to use. Often, printed panels are arranged near coordinating bolts of fabric.

2. Assemble the center panel. Measure the width and the length.

3. Decide on a border width. The side borders will be the width of the border plus seam allowances, by the length of the center panel.

4. The top and bottom borders will be the width of the border plus seam allowances, by the width of the center panel plus the width of the side borders and seam allowances.

For example, your center panel may be 24" x 36" (61 cm x 91.5 cm). If you want a 4" (10 cm) border, then the side borders would measure 4½" x 36½" (11.5 cm x 92.8 cm). The top and bottom borders would measure 4½" x 32½" (11.5 cm x 82.8 cm). The dimensions of the finished quilt would be 32" x 44" (81.5 cm x 112 cm).

Quilted by Lena Colley of New Traditions

WILDLIFE DEER →

A wildlife enthusiast would love a wall hanging like this one. The project doubles as a seasonal accent for fall. Lena Colley wanted to emphasize the woodland theme, so she used a natural thread to quilt the leaves all over the quilt. When she finished quilting, Lena simply bound the quilt with solid black fabric. The back features a coordinating print that goes with this fabric line.

◄ HARBOR LIGHTS

Does someone you know have a beach house or live near the coast? Think how they would enjoy this piece! Since the background suggests a starry night, Lena Colley quilted the project in an allover loops-and-stars pattern. The red-and-black borders are part of the panel. Lena bound and backed the quilt with a star print that coordinates with the background.

Quilted Lena Colley
of New Traditions

Fly Away Home

THIS WALL HANGING LOOKS MORE COMPLEX THAN IT IS. THE MULTIPLE
DUCK SCENES ARE ACTUALLY PART OF ONE CENTRAL PANEL. FOR AN
INTERESTING ACCENT, I ADDED A FLYING GEESE BORDER. USE THIS BOR-
DER TECHNIQUE TO EMBELLISH OTHER PANELS YOU MAY FIND.

Finished Size: 44" x 44"
(112 cm x 112 cm)
Blocks: 76 (2" x 4" [5 cm x 10 cm])
Flying Geese Blocks

MATERIALS

32½" x 32½" (82.8 cm x 82.8 cm)
duck print center panel
¾ yard (0.70 m) cream print for
Flying Geese blocks
152 (2½" [6.3 cm]) squares in
matching sets of two of assorted
prints for Flying Geese blocks
1¼ yards (1.15 m) black dot print for
borders and binding
3 yards (2.75 m) fabric for backing
Crib-size batting

CUTTING
 30 Minutes

Measurements include ¼" (0.6 cm)
seam allowances. Cut crosswise strips
unless otherwise noted.

From the cream print, cut:
• Nine 2½"-wide (6.3 cm) strips.
Cut the strips into 76 (2½" x 4½"
[6.3 cm x 11.5 cm]) rectangles for
the Flying Geese blocks.

From the black dot print, cut:
• Eight 1½"-wide (3.8 cm) lengthwise strips. Cut the strips into two
1½" x 32½" (3.8 cm x 82.8 cm)
top and bottom inner borders, two
1½" x 34½" (3.8 cm x 87.8 cm)
side inner borders, two 1½" x
42½" (3.8 cm x 108.3 cm) top and
bottom outer borders, and two
1½" x 44½" (3.8 cm x 113.3 cm)

**Quilt pieced by Terry
Cates; quilted by New
Traditions**

side outer borders.

- Five 2¼"-wide (5.6 cm-wide) lengthwise strips for the binding.

QUILT ASSEMBLY
⏱ 30 Minutes (per strip) ⏱

1. Referring to the *Diagonal Seams Diagrams*, place one 2½" (6.3 cm) print square atop one end of one 2½" x 4½" (6.3 cm x 11.5 cm) cream rectangle. Stitch diagonally as shown in *Diagram A*. Trim ¼" (0.6 cm) from the stitching *(Diagram B)*.

2. Open and press to reveal the triangle *(Diagram C)*.

3. Repeat on the opposite end with matching 2½" (6.3 cm) print square *(Diagram D)*. Stitch diagonally as shown and trim the excess *(Diagram E)*.

4. Press open to reveal the Flying Geese block *(Diagram F)*.

5. Make 76 Flying Geese blocks.

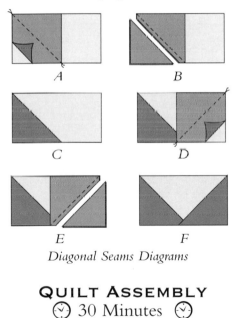

Diagonal Seams Diagrams

QUILT ASSEMBLY
⏱ 30 Minutes ⏱

1. Referring to *Diagram G,* sew the black top and bottom inner borders to the center panel. Sew on the side inner borders.

2. Join 17 Flying Geese units into one strip. Add to the top of the quilt, pointing the units to the right.

3. Repeat for the bottom of the quilt, pointing the units to the left.

4. Join 21 Flying Geese units into one strip. Add to the right side of the quilt, pointing the units down.

5. Repeat for the left side, pointing the units up.

6. Sew the black top and bottom outer borders to the quilt. Sew on the side outer borders *(Diagram H)*.

QUILTING & FINISHING

1. Divide the backing fabric into two 1½-yard (1.40 m) lengths. Cut one piece in half lengthwise. Sew one narrow panel to one side of the wide panel. Press the seam allowances toward the narrow panel. The remaining panel is extra and may be used to make a hanging sleeve.

2. Layer the backing (facedown), the batting (faceup), and the quilt top; baste. Quilt as desired. The quilt shown was quilted with duck and cattail designs.

3. Join 2¼"-wide (5.6 cm-wide) black dot strips into one continuous piece for straight-grain binding. Add the binding to the quilt.

Diagram G

Diagram H

Bases Loaded

THIS SPORTY QUILT WILL THRILL ANY ALL-STAR. CONSIDER ADDING PERSONAL DETAILS, SUCH AS THE ATHLETE'S TEAM NUMBER.

Finished Size: 44" x 44" (112 cm x 112 cm)

Blocks: 4 (18" [46 cm]) Ohio Star Blocks

MATERIALS

¼ yard (0.25 m) large theme for star centers

¾ yard (0.70 m) small print for background (quilt shown has baseball players)

½ yard (0.50 m) light theme for stars (quilt shown has baseballs)

1 yard (0.95 m) red-and-blue print for star points and outer border

¼ yard (0.25 m) blue mottled print for inner border

½ yard (0.50 m) stripe for binding

3 yards (2.75 m) fabric for backing

Crib-size batting

CUTTING

30 Minutes

Measurements include ¼" (0.6 cm) seam allowances. Cut crosswise strips unless otherwise noted.

From the large theme print, cut:
- One 6½"-wide (16.3 cm-wide) strip. Cut the strip into four 6½" (16.3 cm) squares for the star centers.

From the small print, cut:
- Three 6½"-wide (16.3 cm-wide) strips. Cut the strips into 16 (6½" or 16.3 cm) squares for star corners.

From the light theme print, cut:
- Two 7¼"-wide (18.6 cm-wide) strips. Cut the strips into eight 7¼" (18.6 cm) squares. Cut the squares in quarters diagonally to make 32 quarter-square triangles for the star points.

From the red-and-blue print, cut:
- Two 7¼"-wide (18.6 cm-wide) strips. Cut the strips into eight 7¼" (18.6 cm) squares. Cut the squares in quarters diagonally to make 32 quarter-square triangles for star points.
- Four 3"-wide (7.5 cm-wide) strips. Piece as needed to make two 3" x 39½" (7.5 cm x 100.3 cm) side outer borders and two 3" x 44½" (7.5 cm x 113.3 cm) top and bottom outer borders.

From the blue mottled print, cut:
- Four 2"-wide (5 cm-wide) strips. Cut the strips into two 2" x 36½" (5 cm x 92.8 cm) side inner borders and two 2" x 39½" (5 cm x 100.3 cm) top and bottom inner borders.

From the stripe, cut:
- Five 2¼"-wide (5.6 cm-wide) strips for the binding.

BLOCK ASSEMBLY
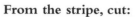
10 Minutes (per block)

1. Join one baseball triangle and one red print triangle as shown in *Diagram A*. Repeat *(Diagram B)*. Join to make one star point unit *(Diagram C)*. Make four star point units *(Diagram D)*.

2. Lay out four star point units, one center square, and four background squares as shown in *Diagram E*. Join into rows; join rows to complete one Ohio Star block *(Diagram F)*.

3. Make four Ohio Star blocks. ⟶

Diagram A

Diagram B

Diagram C

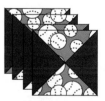

Diagram D

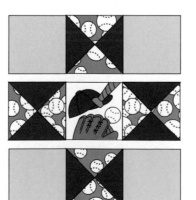

Diagram E

Diagram F

Quilt designed and pieced
by Cindy Wilson; quilted
by New Traditions

Diagram G

QUILT ASSEMBLY
⊙ 30 Minutes ⊙

1. Lay out blocks as shown in *Diagram G.* Join to complete the quilt center.

2. Sew the 2" x 36½" (5 cm x 92.8 cm) blue side inner borders to each quilt side. Sew the 2" x 39½" (5 cm x 100.3 cm) blue top and bottom inner borders to the quilt.

3. Sew the 3" x 39½" (7.5 cm x 100.3 cm) red-and-blue side outer borders to each quilt side. Add the 3" x 44½" (7.5 cm x 113.5 cm) red-and-blue top and bottom outer borders to the quilt.

QUILTING & FINISHING

1. Divide backing fabric into two 1½-yard (1.40 m) lengths. Cut one piece in half lengthwise. Sew one narrow panel to one side of the wide panel. Press the seam allowances toward the narrow panel. The remaining panel is extra and may be used to make a hanging sleeve.

2. Layer the backing (facedown), the batting, and the quilt top (faceup); baste. Quilt as desired. The quilt shown was machine-quilted with an allover loops–and–stars pattern.

3. Join 2¼"-wide (5.6 cm-wide) stripe strips into one continuous piece for straight-grain binding. Add the binding to the quilt.

Dalmatians

SOMETIMES A THEME PRINT INCLUDES SEVERAL DIFFERENT PANELS
IN VARYING SIZES. IN THAT CASE, USE PIECED BLOCKS AND SETTING STRIPS
TO JOIN THE PANELS INTO A QUILT YOU'LL BE PROUD TO GIVE. LOOK FOR
COORDINATING PRINTS TO MATCH YOUR THEME PRINT.

**Quilt designed and made
by Diane Gilley; quilted
by New Traditions**

Finished Size: 33" x 42"
(84 cm x 107 cm)
Blocks: 5 Panels, 2 Pinwheel Blocks

MATERIALS

1 yard [0.95 m] (or more, depending on print) theme print for panels

Six 1½" x 10" (3.8 cm x 25.5 cm) strips assorted red-and-blue print for checkerboard setting strips

One ¾" x 10½" (2 cm x 26.8 cm) strip blue print for bottom right setting strip

One 3" x 11½" (7.5 cm x 29.3 cm) rectangle red print for setting strip

One 3" x 12" (7.5 cm x 30.5 cm) rectangle red-and-blue print for pinwheels

¼ yard (0.25 m) white for setting blocks

¼ yard (0.25 m) gold print for border

¾ yard (0.70 m) blue bandanna print for border and binding

1 yard (0.95 m) fabric for backing

Crib-size batting

Note from Nancy: If you are working with a different theme print than the one I used, you will probably put more time into the initial planning of your quilt. If you sketch out your quilt plan on paper—as I did—you'll find that the assembly goes much faster.

CUTTING
🕐 2 (30-Minute) Periods 🕐

Measurements include ¼" (0.6 cm) seam allowances. Cut crosswise strips unless otherwise noted.

From the theme print, cut:

- Four dog panels and one truck panel. Quilt shown had 9½" x 11½" (24.3 cm x 29.3 cm), 10½" x 11½" (26.8 cm x 29.3 cm), 9½" x 23½" (24.3 cm x 59.8 cm), 9" x 10½" (23 cm x 26.8 cm), and 10½" x 10½" (26.8 cm x 26.8 cm) panels. If you use a different print,

cut the panels as desired and adjust the setting strips as needed.

- Two 1½" x 4½" (3.8 cm x 11.5 cm) rectangles for the bottom pinwheel setting strip.

From the red-and-blue print, cut:

- Four 2⅞" (7.2 cm) squares. Cut the squares in half diagonally to make eight half-square triangles for the pinwheels.

From the white, cut:

- Four 2⅞" (7.2 cm) squares. Cut the squares in half diagonally to make eight half-square triangles for the pinwheels.

- Two 1½"-wide (3.8 cm-wide) strips. Cut the strips into six 1½" x 10" (3.8 cm x 25.5 cm) strips for the checkerboard setting strips.

- One ¾" x 10½" (2 cm x 26.8 cm) strip for the bottom right setting strip.

From the gold print, cut:

- Four 2"-wide (5 cm-wide) strips. Cut the strips into two 2" x 32½" (5 cm x 82.8 cm) side borders and two 2" x 26½" (5 cm x 67.3 cm) top and bottom borders.

From the blue bandanna print, cut:

- Four 4"-wide (10 cm-wide) strips. Cut the strips into two 4" x 35½" (10 cm x 90.3 cm) side borders and two 4" x 33½" (10 cm x 85.3 cm) top and bottom borders.

- Four 2¼"-wide (5.6 cm) strips for the binding.

BLOCK ASSEMBLY
🕐 20 Minutes (per block) 🕐

Note from Nancy: Adjust setting strip widths and lengths as needed as you plan your quilt

1. To make Pinwheels, join one white triangle and one red-and-blue triangle to make one square *(Diagram A)*. Make four squares. Join the squares as shown in *Diagram B* to make one 4½" (11.5

cm) Pinwheel block. Make two Pinwheel blocks. Join as shown. Add one 1½" x 4½" (3.8 cm x 11.5 cm) blue strip to the top and the bottom *(Diagram C)*.

2. To make the checkerboards, join one 1½" (3.8 cm) white strip to one print strip. Cut the joined strips into 35 (1½"-wide or 3.8 cm-wide) segments *(Diagram D)*. Join 11 segments along the sides as shown in *Diagram E* to make one top setting strip. Join 12 segments end to end as shown *(Diagram F)*. Repeat to make a second setting strip. Remove the last white square from the end of each.

Diagram A   *Diagram B*

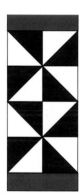

Diagram C

Diagram D

Diagram E

Diagram F

3. Join one white and one blue ¾" x 10½" (2 cm x 26.8 cm) strips to make the bottom right setting strip.

QUILT ASSEMBLY
⏱ 20 Minutes (per step) ⏱

1. Lay out the panels and the setting strips as shown in *Diagram G* or refer to the photo below. Join into rows; join the rows to complete the center.

The center should measure 23½" x 32½" (59.8 cm x 82.8 cm).

2. Sew one 2" x 32½" (5 cm x 82.8 cm) gold side border to each side of the center panel. Add 2" x 26½" (5 cm x 67.3 cm) top and bottom borders.

3. Sew one 4" x 35½" (10 cm x 90.3 cm) blue bandanna side border to each side of the quilt. Add the 4" x 33½" (10 cm x 85.3 cm) top and bottom borders.

QUILTING & FINISHING

1. Layer the backing (facedown), the batting, and the quilt top (faceup); baste. Quilt as desired. The quilt shown was machine-quilted with allover loops and stars.

2. Join 2¼"-wide (5.6 cm-wide) blue bandanna strips into one continuous piece for straight-grain binding. Add the binding to the quilt.

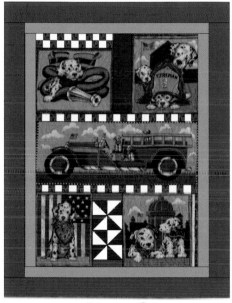

Diagram G

Farmer's Quilt

ALTHOUGH THE DESIGNS CHANGE FROM YEAR TO YEAR, THE JOHN DEERE
PRINTS PRODUCED BY SPRINGS INDUSTRIES REMAIN AMONG
THEIR BEST-SELLERS. WHICHEVER CENTER PANEL YOU CHOOSE,
SPRUCE IT UP WITH A BORDER OF TREES. THESE TREE BLOCKS ARE ALSO
APPROPRIATE FOR WOODLAND PANELS.

Finished Size: 30" x 36"
(76 cm x 91.5 cm)
Blocks: 18 (6" [15 cm]) Tree Blocks

MATERIALS

One 18½" x 24½" (47.3 cm x 62.3
cm) center panel
Nine 5½" (14 cm) squares of assorted greens for trees
One 5" x 7½" (12.5 cm x 19.3 cm)
rectangle brown print for tree trunks
1 yard (0.95 m) tan print for
background
⅓ yard (0.32 m) fabric for binding
1 yard (0.95 m) fabric for backing
One 5" x 7½" (12.5 cm x 19.3 cm)
piece of fusible webbing
One 31" x 37" (78.5 cm x 945 cm)
piece of batting

CUTTING
⏱ 30 Minutes ⏱

Measurements include ¼" (0.6 cm)
seam allowances. Fuse the brown rectangle to the fusible webbing, following the manufacturer's instructions.
From the brown print, cut:
• Nine ½" x 7½" (1.3 cm x 19.3
cm) strips for the tree trunks.
From the tan print, cut:
• Two 5½"-wide (14 cm-wide)
strips. Cut the strips into nine
5½ (14 cm) squares for the tree
trunk backgrounds.
• Four 4"-wide (10 cm-wide) strips.
Cut the strips into 36 (4" or 10

cm) squares. Cut the squares in half
diagonally to make 72 corner triangles for the tree blocks.
From the binding fabric, cut:
• Four 2¼"-wide (5.6 cm-wide) strips
for the binding.

BLOCK ASSEMBLY
⏱ 20 Minutes (per set) ⏱

1. Position one tree trunk strip diagonally across one 5½" (14 cm) tan
print square as shown in *Diagram A*.
Fuse. Repeat to make nine tree trunk
squares.
2. Stack one tree trunk square and
one green square, with the right sides
facing.
3. Draw one diagonal line across the
green square in the opposite direction from the tree trunk. Stitch ¼"
(0.6 cm) from the line on both sides
(Diagram B). As you work, you will
create two blocks *(Photo 1)*.
4. Cut along the drawn line, as
shown in *Photo 2*.
5. Open, press, and square the blocks
to 4¾" (12 cm) to make two Tree
block centers, as shown in *Photo 3*.
6. Add one tan print corner triangle
to each corner of one Tree block
center as shown in *Diagram C*. Trim
the block to 6½" (16.3 cm) to complete one Tree block *(Diagram D)*.
7. Repeat to make 18 Tree blocks.

$\longrightarrow$

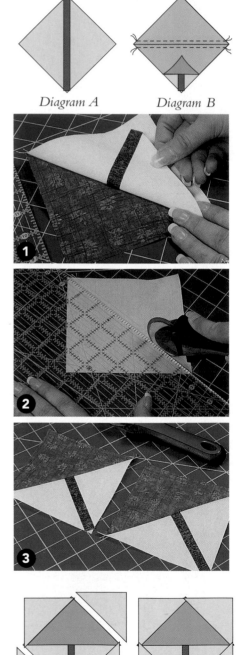

Diagram A   *Diagram B*

Diagram C   *Diagram D*

Quilt designed and
made by Gail Dunn

QUILT ASSEMBLY
⏱ 20 Minutes (per step) ⏱

1. Referring to *Diagram E,* join three Tree blocks to make one side border; repeat for the second side border. Add the borders to each side of the center panel.

2. Join six Tree blocks to make the top border; repeat to make the bottom border. Sew the borders to the quilt.

QUILTING & FINISHING

1. Layer the backing (facedown), the batting, and the quilt top (faceup); baste. Quilt as desired. The quilt shown was outline-quilted around the trees and meander-quilted in the tree backgrounds. The center is quilted by the pattern, and the binding has feather stitching.

2. Join 2¼"-wide (5.6 cm-wide) binding strips into one continuous piece for straight-grain binding. Add the binding to the quilt.

Diagram E

Theme Apron

TAKE ADVANTAGE OF SPECIAL INTEREST PRINTS TO MAKE SMALL PROJECTS. HERE, I USED LEFTOVER FABRIC TO MAKE A GIFT APRON.

Apron by
Gail Dunn

under ½" (1.3 cm) on apron sides and 1" (2.5 cm) at the top and bottom. Stitch in place to secure.

4. To attach the neck ties, take a tuck at each top edge. Sandwich a tie within each tuck and secure by sewing a square with an X (*Diagram C*).

5. To attach the side ties, sew one end to the inside of each apron side. Secure by sewing a square with an X.

Diagram A

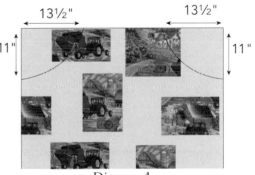
Diagram B

MATERIALS

1 yard (0.95 m) of theme fabric

CUTTING
☽ 20 Minutes ☽

From the theme fabric, cut:
• Three 1½"-wide (3.8 cm-wide) strips for ties. Cut one fabric strip in half to make the ties for the apron neck. Fold the cut edges to meet the center; press. Meet the folded edges to conceal the raw edge. Edgestitch.

From the top of the apron:
• Measure in 13½" (34.3 cm) along

the top and 11" (28 cm) down one side. Using a curved ruler or a large plate, draw a gentle curve from these two points. Repeat on the opposite side (*Diagram A*).
• Cut along the curves to make the arm areas of the apron (*Diagram B*).

ASSEMBLY
☽ 20 Minutes ☽

1. Turn under ¼" (0.6 cm) along all the outer edges of the apron and press. Stitch along the fold to secure.
2. Turn under again and press; turn

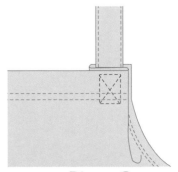

Diagram C

5
Quick Fusible Bias Quilting

NARROW BIAS STRIPS CAN BE USED TO ADD A STAINED-GLASS LOOK TO YOUR APPLIQUÉ QUILTS. Positioning and attaching these strips was once a tedious, time-consuming process. But fusible web and novel notions, such as a Bias Tape Maker, changed all that. Now, it's easy to prepare narrow bias strips, to back them with fusible web, to fuse them in place, and then to secure them with machine stitching.

There's also an even easier solution: QUICK BIAS. This narrow bias trim is prefolded, with a fusible backing already in place. It saves time and is so much fun to use.

If you're new to sewing, you'll find fusible bias extremely easy to use. The *Christmas Tree* wall quilt on page 77 makes a great first project.

So let fusible bias expand your creative potential. THE PROCESS IS SIMPLE, YET THE RESULTS ARE DRAMATIC, with nearly endless design possibilities.

Bias Basics

WHAT IS BIAS?

Woven fabrics are constructed with two sets of yarns *(Diagram A)*. Lengthwise yarns (warp) run parallel to the selvage and stretch very little. Crosswise yarns (weft) run across the fabric from selvage to selvage, at right angles to the lengthwise yarns; they tend to stretch more than lengthwise yarns.

To find a true bias, start at the corner of the fabric. Measure the same distance (for example, 10" [25.5 cm]) from the corner along both the selvage and the crosswise grain. Draw a line connecting those two points to get a true bias *(Diagram B)*.

Bias stretches, even in very stable fabrics. Because of that stretch, bias can be molded and shaped around curves. Bias is often used to finish curved garment edges, such as armholes and necklines. Use narrow bias strips to shape gentle curves and braidlike designs to accent garments and home-decor items. You can also cut bias strips and create bias tape by using a Bias Tape Maker to fold under the raw edges. Then the tape can be shaped, positioned, and stitched in place. I'll show you how in the following pages.

CHOOSING AND TRANSFERRING THE DESIGN

Whenever using bias trim, remember that designs must have **gentle, subtle curves,** rather than hairpin twists and turns. Draw your bias trim design or convert a design from another source.

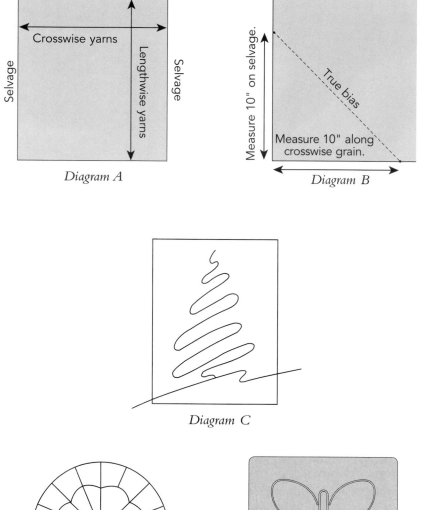

Diagram A

Diagram B

Diagram C

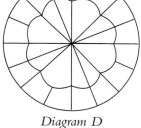

Diagram D

Diagram E

1. Select a design. Here are some options:
• Use a prepared design, such as the tree design on page 81 *(Diagram C)*.

• Draw your own design *(Diagram D)*.
• Adapt a quilting design.
  – Use a quilting stencil that has gentle curves *(Diagram E)*.

74

- Use printed borders designed as quilt borders *(Diagram F)*. For example, many of the Borders Made Easy™ designs from my catalog would be suitable. These designs have adhesive strips on the outer edges to aid in positioning.

2. Transfer the design to the fabric.

• If necessary, enlarge the design to the finished size on paper or on drafting paper, such as Sewable Swedish Drafting Paper. This lightweight nonwoven material is gridded with 1" (2.5 cm) squares with ⅛" (0.3 cm) markings. It's ideal for enlarging patterns *(Diagram G)*.

• Cut a rectangle of fabric to the correct size for the design.

• Place tracing paper, such as Saral® Transfer Paper, on the right side of the fabric.

• Place the design pattern over the transfer paper *(Diagram H)*. Pin all the layers together.

• Trace the design, using a tracing wheel. Use a ruler for straight edges and guide the wheel freehand around curved designs. *(Diagram I)*.

• Remove the transfer paper and the design pattern.

PREPARING BIAS TRIM

For a custom look, make your own trim from a fabric of your choice. Or for an easy alternative, use ready-made Quick Bias.

1. Create the bias trim.

• Cut bias strips.

- Align the 45° angle of a quilting ruler along the fabric selvage; cut it with a rotary cutter. Or form a true bias, as detailed at left, and cut along the line *(Diagram J)*.

- Cut ½" (1.3 cm) strips along the bias edge *(Diagram K)*.

• Join the bias strips.

- Determine the length of bias needed for the project by placing

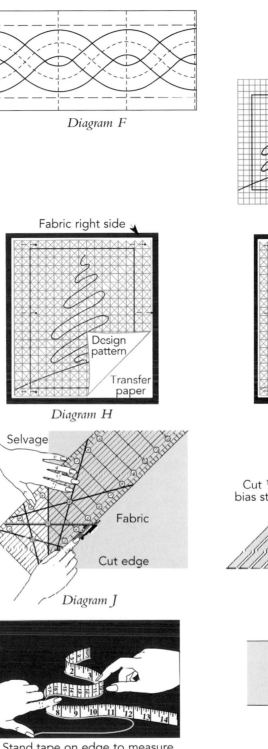

Diagram F

Fabric right side

Design pattern

Transfer paper

Diagram H

Selvage

Fabric

Cut edge

Diagram J

Stand tape on edge to measure design length.
Diagram L

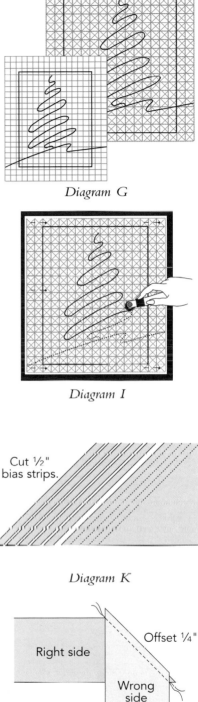

Diagram G

Diagram I

Cut ½" bias strips.

Diagram K

Right side

Offset ¼"

Wrong side

Diagram M

a tape measure along the edge of the design and measure the length *(Diagram L)*.

- Meet the short ends of two strips, with the right sides together; offsett the ends by approximately

¼" (0.6 cm). Small triangles will extend on each edge.

- Mark a diagonal line from corner to corner; stitch along the line, using a short stitch length *(Diagram M)*. →

- Press the seam open; if desired, trim the triangle extensions (*Diagram O*).
- Join additional strips to obtain the necessary length of bias stripping.
• Create ¼" (0.6 cm) bias tape.
  - Insert the ½" (1.3 cm) bias strip into the wide end of a ¼" (0.6 cm) Bias Tape Maker.
  - Use a pin to advance the fabric through the tool. Press the fabric as it comes through the Bias Tape Maker (*Diagram P*).

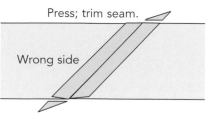

Press; trim seam.

Wrong side

Diagram O

Diagram P

Note from Nancy: When making tape from narrow bias strips, it's important to work in small increments—no more than a 1" (2.5 cm) length at a time. This helps ensure that the completed tape will be smooth and of a uniform width.

- When nearing a seam, press the seam allowances away from the Bias Tape Maker. As the seam goes through the tool, you may need to advance and to press in even shorter increments to prevent the seam allowances from buckling

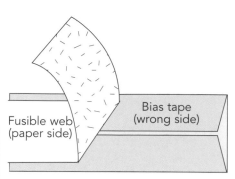

Fusible web (paper side)

Bias tape (wrong side)

Diagram Q

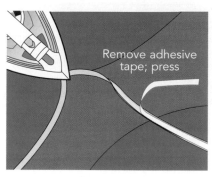

Remove adhesive tape; press

Diagram R

and creating a taper of an uneven width.
• Add fusible web to the bias tape.
  - Cut scant ¼" (0.6 cm) strips from a fusible web, such as HeatBond® Lite Iron-On Adhesive.
  - Position the fusible web on the wrong side of the bias tape. Press, fusing the web to the tape (*Diagram Q*).

2. As an easy alternative, use ready-made Quick Bias. Quick Bias is a prefolded, preshrunk ¼" (0.6 cm) bias tape with finished edges. It has a fusible backing that simplifies positioning and stitching. It's available in a wide variety of colors, including metallic variations. The stitched tape, which is both machine washable and dry cleanable, is a great time- and labor-saver (*Diagram R*).

Both of these quilts were made with Quick Bias. and make ideal holiday projects. Once the design is fused in place, you can quickly machine-quilt the layers.

Instructions begin on page 83.

Christmas Tree Wall Quilt

THIS CONTEMPORARY WALL HANGING, DESIGNED BY DONNA FENSKE, WAS PRODUCED WITH QUICK FUSING AND EDGESTITCHING. IT'S A GREAT FIRST PROJECT FOR USING FUSIBLE BIAS STRIPS. ENLARGE THE PATTERN FOUND ON PAGE 81 OR DRAW A TREE FREEHAND.

Quilt designed by
Donna Fenske, made
by Terry Cates

MATERIALS

18" x 22" (46 cm x 56 cm) piece
background fabric

18" x 22" (46 cm x 56 cm) piece
each of batting and backing fabric

4¼ yards (3.9 m) of ¼" (0.6 cm) bias
tape (Quick Bias or custom–made
trim)

¼ yard (0.25 m) fabric for binding

Star button (optional)

QUILT ASSEMBLY
🕐 30 Minutes 🕐

1. Enlarge the pattern on page 81 or
draw a tree freehand. Trace the tree
design onto the fabric as detailed on
pages 74 and 75 *(Diagram A).*

Diagram A

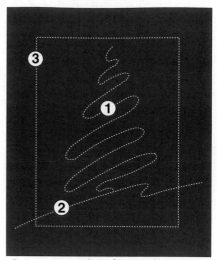

Determine order of tape placement.
Diagram B

🕐 30 Minutes 🕐

2. Determine the order in which
the tape will be applied to various
portions of the design.

• Arrange the tape so that the ends
of the first piece of tape will be hid-
den by subsequent lines of tape.

• Referring to *Diagram B,* apply the
bias tape in this order:

   – Position and stitch the bias tape
to the tree first (1).

   – Next, position and stitch the
bias tape to the horizon line (2).

   – Finally, position and stitch the
bias tape to the border (3).

🕐 30 Minutes 🕐

3. Apply the fusible tape to the
traced tree design.

• Peel off the paper backing from the
fusible bias tape *(Diagram C).* Position
the bias tape over the marked design
and press with a steam iron *(Diagram D).*

• At the curves, gently shape the bias
tape *(Diagram E).* If the curves are
narrow and/or sharp, the bias may
form small tucks. Take your time in
shaping and pressing the tape; the

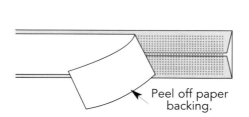

Peel off paper
backing.

Diagram C

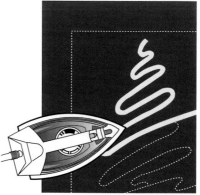

Diagram D

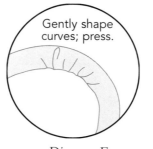

Gently shape
curves; press.

Diagram E

Fold under tape
to clean-finish
end.

Diagram F

finished look is determined now.

• At the top of the tree design, fold
the tape under to clean-finish the
tape end *(Diagram F).*

• If you don't like the tree shape, pull off
the tape and repress.

4. Layer the quilt.

• Cut the backing and the batting to
the same size as the quilt top.

• Place the backing on a flat surface,
with the wrong side up.

• Place the batting over the backing.

• Place the quilt, with the right side up, on top of the batting *(Diagram G)*.
• Pin all the layers together, starting in the middle of the fabric and working toward the outer edges *(Diagram H)*.

☉ 30 Minutes ☉

5. Stitch the tree in place.
• Select a thread for the top of the machine; match the color to the fusible bias tape. Select a needle that corresponds with the thread. With metallic thread, use a metallic needle; with cotton thread, use a universal or sharp needle; and with rayon machine embroidery thread, use a machine embroidery needle.
• Thread the bobbin with lightweight bobbin thread or all-purpose thread.
• Set the machine for 12 to 15 stitches per inch (2.0). The short stitch length makes it easy to manipulate and to stitch curves.
• Stitch along each side of the fusible bias tape *(Diagram I)*.
   - Stop with the needle in the fabric when pivoting or turning at curves.
   - Stitch slowly around curves for better control; reserve fast stitching for straight sections.
• Optional: Replace the conventional presser foot with an open toe foot.
   - The opening in the foot is ¼" (0.6 cm), precisely right for guiding the fusible bias tape.
   - Move the needle position to the right so that it follows the edge of the tape.
   - Guide the foot along the tape. The stitching will automatically follow along the edge *(Diagram J)*.
   • Repeat, moving the needle position to the left and stitching along the left edge of the tape *(Diagram K)*.
6. Repeat, positioning and stitching the horizon line in place *(Diagram L)*.

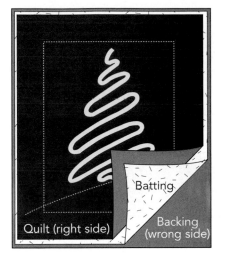

Diagram G

Pin layers together.
Diagram H

Diagram I

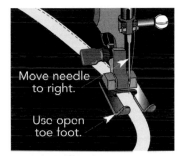

Move needle to right.
Use open toe foot.
Diagram J

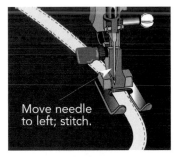

Move needle to left; stitch.
Diagram K

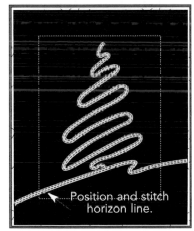

Position and stitch horizon line.
Diagram L

☉ 20 Minutes ☉

7. Position and stitch the fusible bias tape borders in place.
• Mark the position for the borders.
• Use ¼" (0.6 cm) ready-made Quick Bias or create ¼" (0.6 cm) or ½" (1.3 cm) fusible bias.

• To make ½" (1.3 cm) fusible bias, cut 1" (2.5 cm) bias strips and use a ½" (1.3 cm) Bias Tape Maker. The wider ½" (1.3 cm) fusible bias can be used for such straight edges as borders, but it will not shape well around curves.

⟶

• Cut one end of the fusible bias at a 90° angle. Position the cut edge at one corner (Diagram M).

• Position and press the fusible bias from the first corner to the next corner along the traced line. Check with a ruler to ensure that the line is straight (Diagram N); if not, remove that section with a stiletto or the tip of a pin and reposition the trim.

• Miter the corner.

  - Fold the bias tape back at the corner. Place a pin at the outer corner (Diagram O).

  - Refold the tape so that the lengthwise edge aligns with the fold and the tape follows the marked line, forming a point at the pin. This miters the corner (Diagram P).

  - Repeat, positioning the tape and pressing and mitering the remaining corners.

  - At the final corner, fold the tape under at a 45° angle; trim the excess. Fuse the tape over the beginning of the bias tape (Diagram Q).

• Stitch the tape in place, following the process detailed on page 79.

8. Bind the outer edges of the quilt.

• Square the quilt, measuring from the top to the bottom, from the right to the left, and from corner to corner (Diagram R).

• Bind the edges, using your favorite technique. If you used custom-made bias tape for the bias trim in the design, use that same fabric for the binding; if you used ready-made Quick Bias for the bias trim, use the background fabric for the binding (Diagram S).

9. Optional: Add a star button for embellishment.

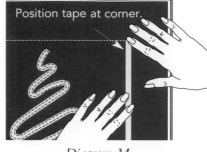

Position tape at corner.

Diagram M

Use ruler to keep tape positioned in a straight line.

Diagram N

Fold back bias tape; place pin at corner.

Diagram O

Miter corner; align tape along next line.

Diagram P

Fold under tape end at 45° angle.

Diagram Q

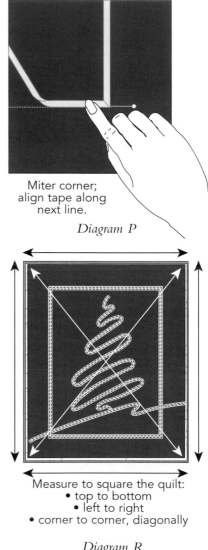

Measure to square the quilt:
• top to bottom
• left to right
• corner to corner, diagonally

Diagram R

Add button star (optional).

Add binding.

Diagram S

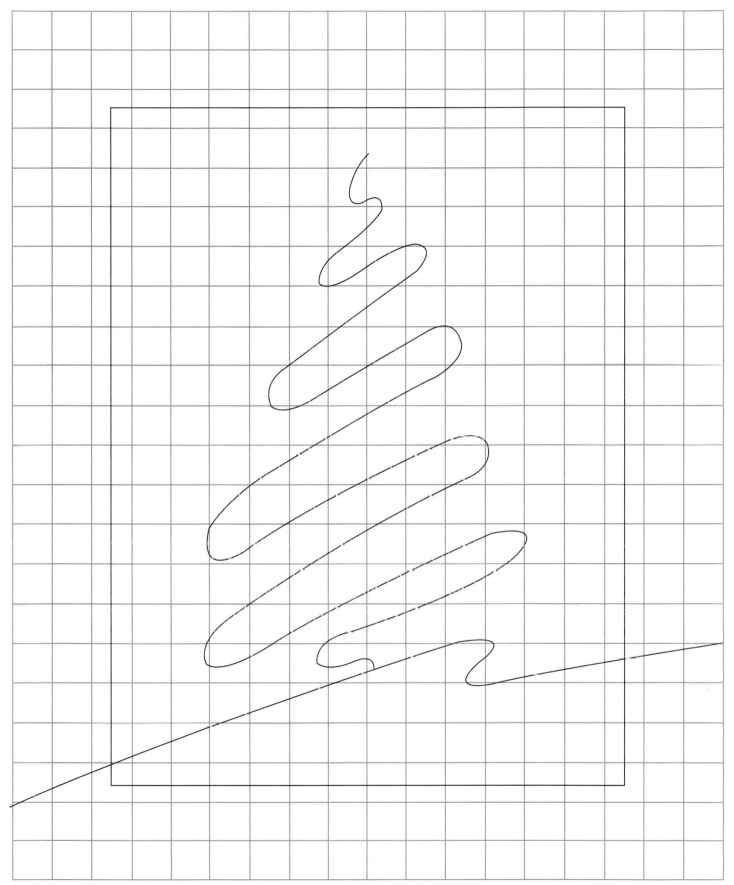

Tree Pattern
Enlarge design 252%.
1 square = 1"

Stained-glass Bloom

THIS BEAUTIFUL STAINED-GLASS QUILT DESIGN IS SO EASY
TO MAKE WITH QUICK BIAS. THE FUSIBLE TAPE IS A REAL
TIME-SAVER, AS IT SHAPES EASILY AROUND CURVES
AND CORNERS. PLUS, AFTER YOU FUSE THE TAPE TO THE PROJECT,
YOU CAN STITCH IT IN PLACE WITHOUT PINNING.

Quilt designed by
Gretchen Hudock;
made by Terry Cates

Finished Size: 24" x 24"
(61 cm x 61 cm)

MATERIALS

5" (12.5 cm) square scrap gold print for center

½ yard (0.50 m) theme print

27" (68.5 cm) square fabric for backing

½ yard (0.50 m) blue print for inner borders and outer petals

⅛ yard (0.15 m) purple fabric for inner petals

27" (68 cm) square of batting

5½-yard (5.05 m) spool Quick Bias Sol-u-web™

HELPFUL NOTIONS

Lightracer™

Soapstone Fabric Marker

Medeira Monofil Thread

Size 1 Curved Basting Pins

Appliqué Pressing Sheet

CUTTING
⊙ 30 Minutes ⊙

Patterns are on page 85.

1. Make templates for the inner petal, the outer petal, and the center circle. Lay out and cut the quilt pieces as shown in *Diagram A*.

2. From Sol-u-web, cut one center circle and one ½" x 9" (1.3 cm x 23 cm) strip. Cut the strip into ½" (1.3 cm) lengths.

TRANSFERRING
THE DESIGN
⊙ 30 Minutes ⊙

4. Transfer the design to the 18" (46 cm) square.

• Fold the base fabric into quarters and lightly press the folds; unfold the fabric.

• Place the fabric over the paper block pattern, matching the fabric folds with the center and the horizontal and

vertical pattern lines. (Use a light table or a window to help to see the lines.)

5. Trace the outline of the design onto the fabric with a marking tool, repeating the design for each quarter of the circle *(Diagram B)*.

QUILT ASSEMBLY
⊙ 30 Minutes (per set) ⊙

6. Assemble the flower design on the base fabric.

• Position the purple inner petals with

the cut edges touching *(Diagram C)*.

• Position and apply the blue outer petals *(Diagram D)*.

• Insert a ½" (1.3 cm) square of Sol-u-web under each appliqué piece; press the petals in place.

7. Apply Quick Bias and the center circle.

• For each layer, position the tape over the raw edges of the appliqué, fuse with an iron, and edgestitch along both edges of the tape. Or blindhem-stitch with a clear thread.

⟶

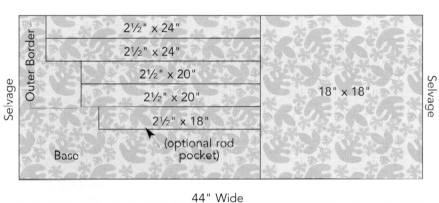

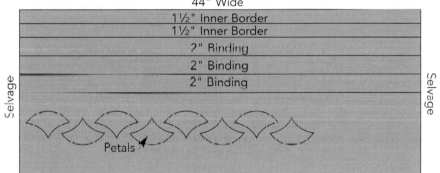

Diagram A

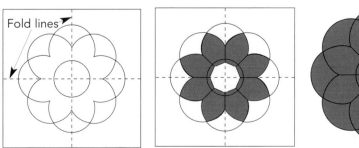

Transfer design to base fabric.   Position inner petals.   Position outer petals.

Diagram B   *Diagram C*   *Diagram D*

- Position the Quick Bias circle first *(Diagram E)*.

- Cut eight 3½" (9 cm) lengths of Quick Bias. Position them over the intersections of the inner petals, overlapping the circle *(Diagram F)*.

- Form the first scallop series, overlapping the tape at the intersections and mitering the corners *(Diagram G)*.

- Repeat for the second scallop *(Diagram H)*.

• Stitch Sol-u-web to the right side of the center circle fabric ¼" (0.6 cm) from the edge; trim the excess. Slit the Sol-u-web and turn the circle right side out. Press the circle with the Sol-u-web side toward the appliqué pressing sheet; cool. Place in the center of the petals, covering the raw ends of Quick Bias; fuse and edgestitch *(Diagram H)*.

8. Join the border strips to the block.

• Inner border (blue print)

- Cut and stitch 18" (46 cm) strips onto opposite sides of the quilt square. Press the seams toward the border.

- Cut and stitch 20" (51 cm) strips to the top and the bottom; press the seams toward the border *(Diagram I)*.

• Outer border (theme print)

- Repeat the steps, using 20" (51 cm) and 24" (61 cm) strips.

QUILTING & FINISHING

9. Quilt the block.

• Layer the backing (facedown), the batting, and the quilt top (faceup) *(Diagram J)*. Baste.

• Quilt the design.

• Trim the edges of the backing and the batting even with the quilt top. Baste the edges together.

10. Apply the binding (theme print).

• Join 2" (5 cm) strips together at the short ends.

• Fold the binding in half lengthwise,

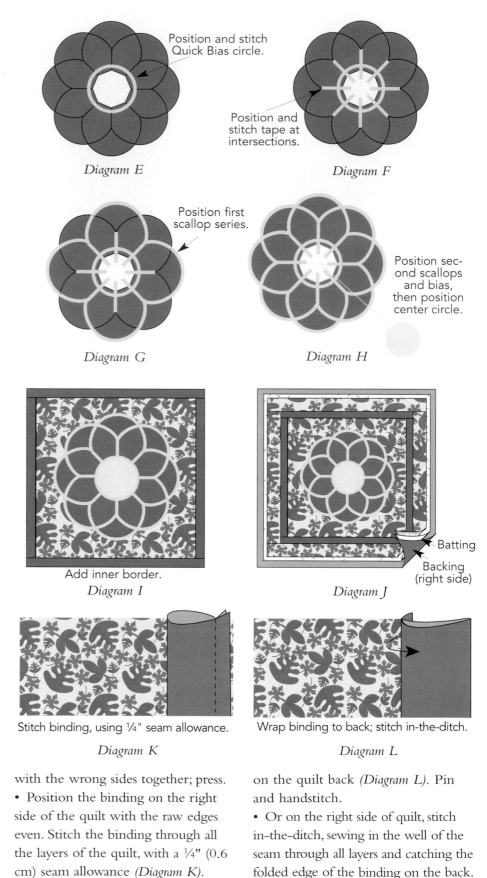

Position and stitch Quick Bias circle.

Diagram E

Position and stitch tape at intersections.

Diagram F

Position first scallop series.

Diagram G

Position second scallops and bias, then position center circle.

Diagram H

Add inner border.
Diagram I

Batting
Backing (right side)
Diagram J

Stitch binding, using ¼" seam allowance.
Diagram K

Wrap binding to back; stitch in-the-ditch.
Diagram L

with the wrong sides together; press.

• Position the binding on the right side of the quilt with the raw edges even. Stitch the binding through all the layers of the quilt, with a ¼" (0.6 cm) seam allowance *(Diagram K)*.

• Fold the binding to the back over the raw edges, covering the seam line

on the quilt back *(Diagram L)*. Pin and handstitch.

• Or on the right side of quilt, stitch in-the-ditch, sewing in the well of the seam through all layers and catching the folded edge of the binding on the back.

11. To hang the quilt, add a rod pocket or tabs, using your favorite technique.

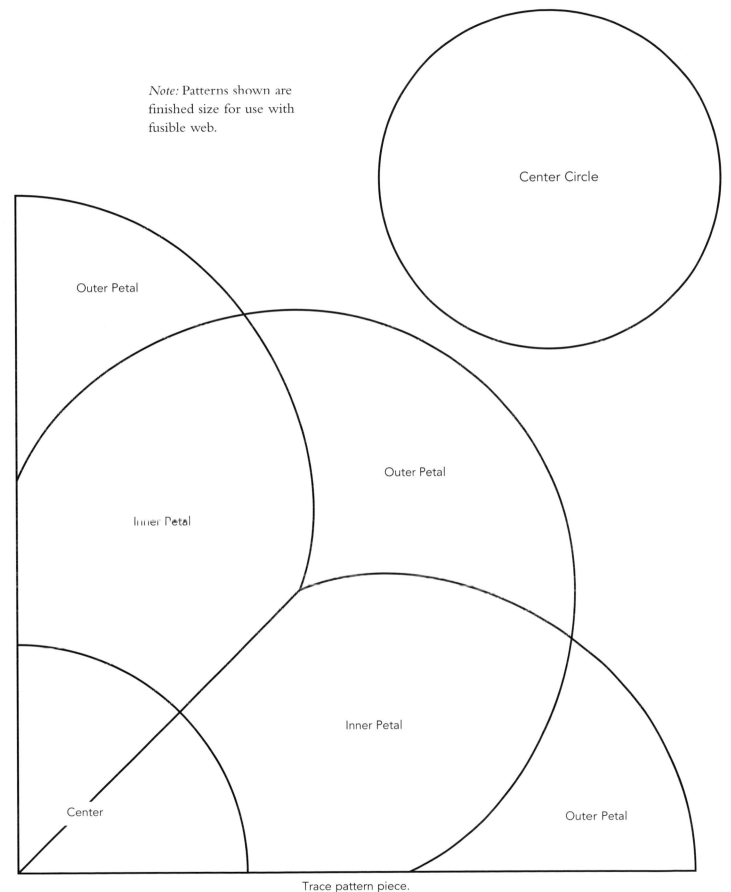

Note: Patterns shown are finished size for use with fusible web.

Center Circle

Outer Petal

Outer Petal

Inner Petal

Inner Petal

Center

Outer Petal

Trace pattern piece.
(¼ of design)

6
Create a Keepsake

Memories become more precious as the years go by. IF YOU'RE LIKE ME, YOU'LL DO ALL YOU CAN TO PRESERVE SPECIAL MOMENTS. Traditionally, we use photos and scrapbooks to capture and to record important events, but now it's just as easy to showcase your memories on fabric.

IN THIS CHAPTER, DISCOVER THE BASICS OF USING PHOTO TRANSFER PAPER to transfer photocopies of black-and-white or color photos, artwork, and printed materials to fabric. Each project represents a method of remembering those treasured moments from the past and creating a memorable keepsake that will be cherished in the future.

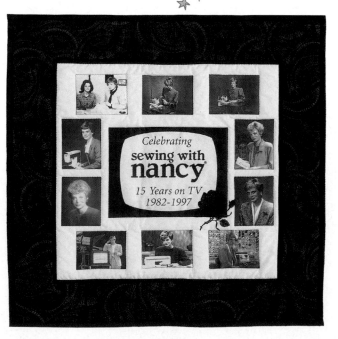

Photo Transfer Basics

TRANSFERRING PHOTOS TO FABRIC IS A RELATIVELY NEW CONCEPT, BUT IT'S SO EASY! AND YOUR PHOTOS ARE NOT DAMAGED IN ANY WAY. HERE ARE A FEW IDEAS TO GET YOU STARTED.

1. Select color and/or black-and-white photos.

2. Arrange the photos on an 8½" x 11" (21.8 cm x 28 cm) sheet of plain white paper.

• Group photos of similar colorations on one sheet.

• Position the photos as close together as possible; there's no need to leave space between them *(Diagram A)*.

3. Copy the photos onto special transfer paper.

• Photo Transfer Paper is available for both color copiers and ink jet printers. Be sure to select the type designed for color copiers (for example, Photo Quilts Transfer Paper) when you're transferring photos.

• Use a color copier, even if you're working with black-and-white photos.

• Select the mirror image button on the copier. If the photos contain text or numbers, such items would appear backwards in the completed transfer without mirror imaging *(Diagram B)*.

• Make a test copy. On many copiers, it's possible to adjust the coloration.

Note from Nancy: I've found that transfers are better while the color copier is still cool, rather than after it has been used throughout the day.

• Make a color copy of each photo that you wish to preserve on fabric.

4. Transfer the photocopied images to fabric.

• Set a dry iron to a "cotton" setting. **Do not** use steam.

• Cut the images apart. Use entire photos *(Diagram C)* or crop just the portions you want.

• Select a premium-quality cotton fabric, such as Southern Belle Broadcloth. This tightly woven 200-count combed cotton fabric has a very smooth surface with minimal flecks, which is important in avoiding blemishes in the transferred photos.

• For each, place the photocopy facedown on the right side of the fabric, leaving sufficient fabric around the outer edges of the photo for the seam allowances. Press for 30 seconds, applying as much pressure as possible *(Diagram D)*. Do not move the iron back and forth.

Note from Nancy: Pressing on a wooden surface, rather than a padded one, seems to improve results. Slip a pillowcase or other piece of fabric over the ironing board and press. It's best to work with photos no larger than the iron soleplate so that you can maintain an even, consistent heat on the entire surface. If your photos are larger than the soleplate, consider using a professional press, such as the Euro-Pro® Press and Stand, which provides an even temperature over the entire photo.

8½"

11"

Diagram A

Diagram B

Original photo

Mirror image

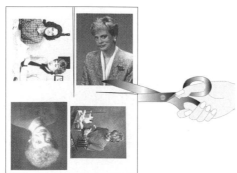
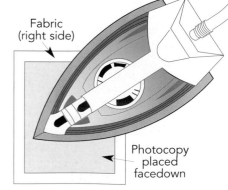

Diagram C

Fabric (right side)

Photocopy placed facedown

Diagram D

• Peel off the paper while it is hot *(Diagram E)*. If the paper does not peel away smoothly, place the paper back down and press for 30 seconds more. If the fabric appears distorted after you remove the paper, turn the transfer over and place the fabric right side down on the ironing board. Steam the fabric, and it should return to its original flat shape.

• Optional: If the transfer will be used as an appliqué, press paper-backed fusible web, such as HeatnBond® Lite Iron-On Adhesive or pressure-sensitive Steam-a-Seam 2®, to the wrong side of the fabric after transferring the photo *(Diagram F)*. Do not remove the paper backing until you're ready to add the appliqué to your project.

5. Use the same techniques to transfer photos to other fabric projects. For example, add a vacation photo to a T-shirt or a work photo to a tote bag *(Diagram G)*.

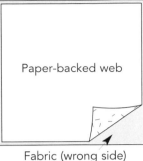

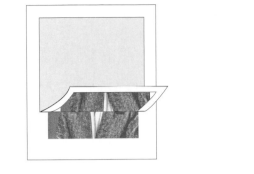

Diagram E

Paper-backed web

Fabric (wrong side)
Diagram F

Diagram G

Note from Nancy: *June Tailor now has a product called Computer Printer Fabric (available through our catalog) that allows you to print images from your ink jet computer directly onto this special fabric. Chemicals in the fabric make the images colorfast. This allows you to work with scanned photos or photos taken with a digital camera.*

Quilt by Gretchen Hudock

Use photo transfer images within traditional quilt blocks for a modern twist. This quilt chronicles the life of Beth Hudock, Gretchen's daughter.

Christmas Photo Quilt

PRESERVE CHRISTMAS MEMORIES IN A PHOTO TRANSFER QUILT.
FEATURE A FOLK-ART CHRISTMAS TREE IN THE CENTER AND PLACE
PHOTOS IN THE BORDERS. EACH YEAR YOU CAN ADD NEW
PHOTOS TO THE BORDERS, CREATING A LASTING KEEPSAKE.

Finished Size: 18½" x 22½"
(47.3 cm x 57.3 cm)

MATERIALS

One 8½" x 16½" (21.8 cm x 41.8 cm) blue snowflake print for center panel
⅝ yard (0.60 m) solid coordinating fabric for borders and backing
⅝ yard (0.60 m) batting
¼ yard (0.25 m) coordinating print for binding
Scraps of green print for holly leaves
Buttons and charms for accents
Steam-a-Seam 2®

CUTTING
⏱ 10 Minutes ⏱

Refer to *Cutting Diagram.*
From the solid coordinating fabric, cut:
• One 18½" x 22½" (47.3 cm x 57.3 cm) piece for backing.
• Two 5½" x 16½" (14 cm x 41.8 cm) side borders.
• Two 3½" x 12½" (9 cm x 31.8 cm) top and bottom borders.

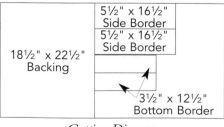

	5½" x 16½" Side Border
18½" x 22½" Backing	5½" x 16½" Side Border
	3½" x 12½" Bottom Border

Cutting Diagram

From the binding fabric, cut:
• Three 2¼"-wide strips for binding.

QUILT ASSEMBLY
⏱ 30 Minutes ⏱

1. Add penstitching to the top and bottom borders.

> *Note from Nancy:* Penstitching involves drawing short, dashed lines that resemble stitching lines, using a permanent, fabric-safe pen.

• Cut pieces of paper to the size of the top and bottom borders. Fold the papers in half, meeting the short ends, to find the center *(Diagram A).*
• Print the desired phrases onto the panels, centering the words *(Diagram B).*

> *Note from Nancy:* If you have a computer, you can center the text easily or even experiment with some fun fonts.

• Place printed paper pieces on a light table *(Diagram C).*
• Fold the top and bottom borders in half, meeting the short ends. Mark the center of each with a pin.
• Unfold the borders and place them over the paper patterns, matching the centers.
• Penstitch the lettering, using a .05 Pigma Pen *(Diagram D).*

> *Note from Nancy:* Pigma pens will not fade, smear, or feather when dry. The ink is waterproof and fadeproof against sunlight and ultraviolet light. As an alternative, add text with sewing machine embroidery stitches.

$\longrightarrow$

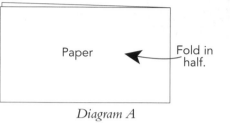

Paper — Fold in half.

Diagram A

Home for the Holidays

Diagram B

Diagram C

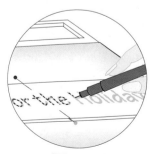

Diagram D

Quilt designed
and made by
Kate Bashynski

2. Add the tree appliqué. (Patterns are on the opposite page.)

• Trace the sections of the appliqué onto Steam-a-Seam 2, adding a ¼" (0.6 cm) seam allowance to each edge *(Diagram E)*.

• Meet the paper side of Steam-a-Seam 2 to the right side of the fabric. For each piece, stitch around the design. Trim to within ¼" (0.6 cm) of the stitching line *(Diagram F)*.

• Fold the Steam-a-Seam 2 seam allowance toward the center of the appliqué along the stitching lines; crease and finger-press *(Diagram G)*.

• Remove the paper backing (but not the interfacing/adhesive) between the raw edges and the stitching line. Trim close to the stitching line *(Diagram H)*.

• Slit the paper backing from the center to each corner *(Diagram I)*.

• Turn the appliqué piece right side out, using a Bamboo Presser & Creaser to shape the corners *(Diagram J)*.

• Remove the paper backing; position the appliqué piece on the wall quilt. (Steam-a-Seam 2 temporarily secures the appliqué for stitching.) Repeat for all the appliqué pieces.

• Sew the appliqué piece to the quilt, using monofilament thread and a sewing machine blindhem stitch *(Diagram K)*.

• Embellish the tree with buttons and charms. Add red buttons for holly berries.

3. Sew the side borders to the quilt; then sew the top and bottom borders.

QUILTING & FINISHING

1. Layer the backing (facedown), the batting, and the quilt top (faceup); baste.

2. Stitch in-the-ditch around the center panel.

3. Add the binding to the quilt.

4. Each year, add a photo transfer to the quilt.

• Select appropriate fabric for the photo transfers. Purchase sufficient fabric to reserve some for future years.

• Transfer the photos to the fabric as detailed on pages 88 and 89. Back the transferred photos with paper-backed fusible web.

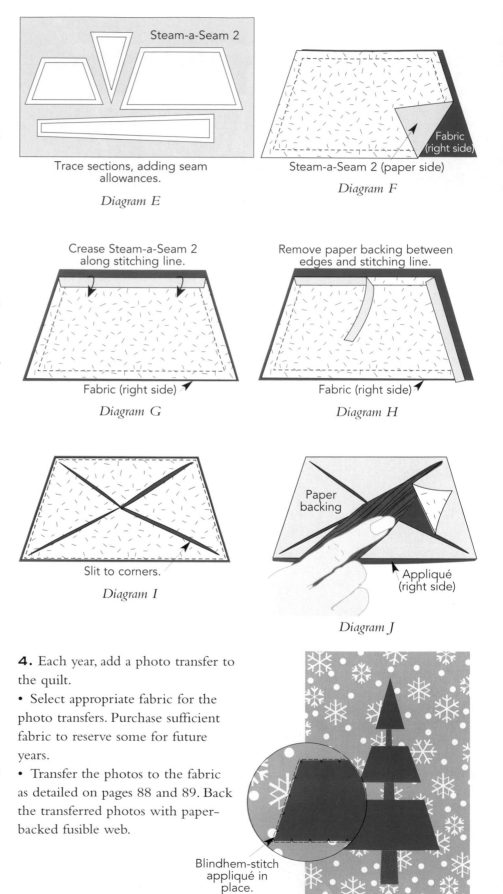

Steam-a-Seam 2

Trace sections, adding seam allowances.

Diagram E

Fabric (right side)

Steam-a-Seam 2 (paper side)

Diagram F

Crease Steam-a-Seam 2 along stitching line.

Fabric (right side)

Diagram G

Remove paper backing between edges and stitching line.

Fabric (right side)

Diagram H

Slit to corners.

Diagram I

Paper backing

Appliqué (right side)

Diagram J

Blindhem-stitch appliqué in place.

Diagram K

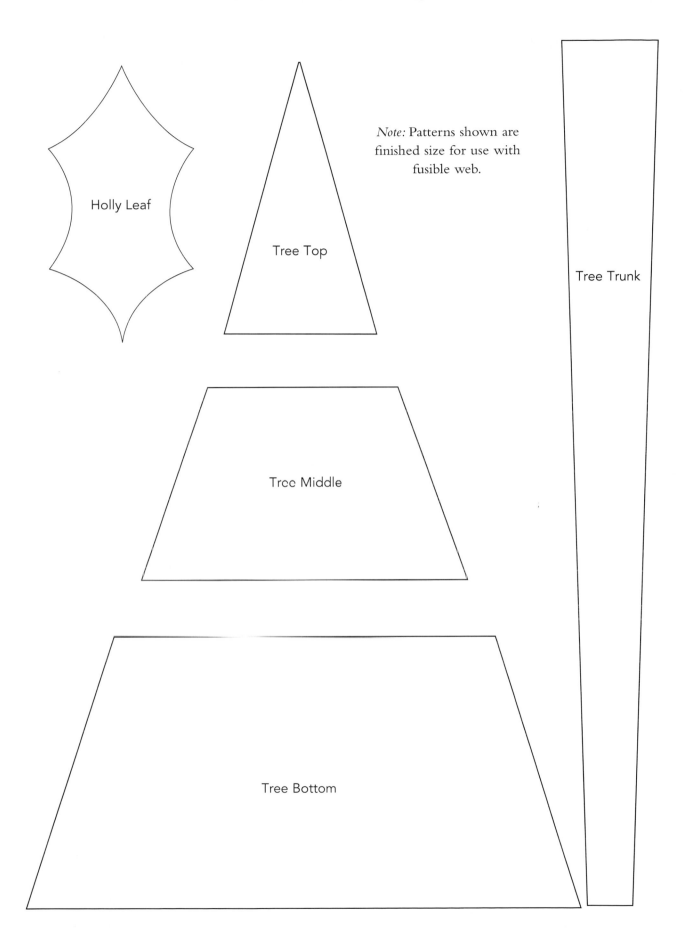

Holly Leaf

Tree Top

Note: Patterns shown are finished size for use with fusible web.

Tree Trunk

Tree Middle

Tree Bottom

Childhood Memories Quilt

THIS QUILT, CREATED BY NANCY'S NOTIONS® QUILTING CONSULTANT
GRETCHEN HUDOCK, RECORDS HER SON JOHN'S CHILDHOOD. GRETCHEN
USED TASTEFUL FABRIC COLORS, CONSISTENT PHOTO SIZES, AND A
LOG CABIN DESIGN TO FASHION THIS QUILT.

PREPARATION

1. Use photos of a similar size. (School photos are ideal, since they generally have a consistent size.) If photos are not the same size, crop portions so that they all match.

2. Transfer the photos to the fabric as detailed on pages 88 and 89.

3. Cut the transferred photo fabrics to a uniform block size, leaving ¼" (0.6 cm) seam allowances.

4. Choose fabrics for the Log Cabin design.

• Select two light shades, with one slightly darker than the other. Also select two dark shades, again with one slightly darker than the other.

• Choose fabrics that are not "busy." Fabrics should enhance and frame the photos, rather than detract or conflict with them.

• Determine the strip width, based on the size of the photos. The photos on the quilt shown were 3½" (9 cm) square. The strips were cut 1½" (3.8 cm) for a 1" (2.5 cm) finished strip width after seam allowances.

QUILT ASSEMBLY

5. Stitch the strips to the photo, using a variation of the Log Cabin design. The design pictured is Fields and Furrows.

• Arrange the photos in chronological order.

• Starting with the lightest fabric strip on the *right* of the first photo, add strips in the colorations shown. Repeat for the first and third blocks of the top, middle, and bottom rows, and the second and fourth blocks of the second and fourth rows.

• Stitch the remaining blocks, starting with the lightest fabric strip on the *left* of the photo and following the sequence and the coloration as shown in the photo at left.

• Arrange the blocks, alternating them as shown, to create the Fields and Furrows design.

Quilt designed and made by Gretchen Hudock for her son John

Anniversary Quilts

TO ENSURE THAT FUTURE GENERATIONS WILL KNOW WHO HOLDS HONORED PLACES ON YOUR QUILTS, USE YOUR COMPUTER TO ADD BIOGRAPHICAL INFORMATION.

Donna Fenske, who works with production of *Sewing With Nancy®*, designed the anniversary quilts below. To create a consistent look, she trimmed the unwanted backgrounds and placed the cutouts on a common background (in this case, stationery).

Then she photocopied the mounted photos onto Photo Transfer Paper.

To add genealogy information, Donna used her computer to print the text she wanted to appear on her quilt. Then she photocopied the typed information, along with the

appropriate photograph, onto Photo Transfer Paper. (Remember to make a mirror image so that the type appears correctly on the completed transfer.) If you have a scanner, you can scan photos first and then type and center text under them.

Quilts designed and made by Donna Fenske

Remember that when you are working with Photo Transfer Paper, you should always use a color copier—even if your photos are black and white.

Special Occasion Quilt

REMEMBER THAT ANNIVERSARIES CAN ALSO APPLY TO CAREER MILESTONES.
TO CELEBRATE NANCY ZIEMAN'S FIFTEENTH YEAR OF BEING ON TELEVISION,
HER STAFF MADE HER A PHOTO TRANSFER QUILT, DOCUMENTING
VARIOUS PHASES IN NANCY'S CAREER. THE CENTER PANEL
WAS COMPUTER-GENERATED AND THEN TRANSFERRED ONTO FABRIC.

1. Select the photos.

> *Note from Nancy: Arrange your photos on a flannel board or fleece to determine which photos to use and how to group them. You may modify this arrangement in the finished quilt, but it gives you a starting point. Watch for a balance of color and size. Try grouping smaller photos by theme and treating them as a single unit.*

2. Follow the instructions on pages 88 and 89 for photo transfer.

3. Using a computer, create the words to transfer.

• Type and print out the lettering to the desired finished size.

4. Photocopy a mirror image of the words.

• Treat the reverse lettering as a photo. Transfer the lettering to the transfer paper. If the color copier has mirror image capacity, simply print out the lettering and then push the mirror image button when you photocopy the image onto the Photo Transfer Paper *(Diagram)*.

5. Arrange the photo transfer images as desired on a large piece of muslin.

6. Choose a coordinating print and add borders. In the quilt shown, there is a skinny red inner border and a large gray print outer border. The binding is red, to match the inner border.

Diagram

Celebrating

sewing with nancy®

15 Years on TV
1982-1997

**Quilt designed and made by
staff of Sewing with Nancy**

*Consider adding other embellishments, such as the rose shown in this quilt. You can enhance a design with
machine- or hand-embroidered details, or fuse purchased appliqué shapes onto the quilt.*

7
Crazy Quilting

IS THERE A SEWING ENTHUSIAST AMONG US WHO DOESN'T HAVE BOXES OF FABRIC SCRAPS? One of the best ways to use up those pieces is to make a crazy quilt or a small project with crazy piecing. Using this technique, the size or the shapes of your scraps really doesn't matter.

Today's sewing machines allow us to make a number of embellishing stitches that used to take days to do by hand. IF YOU OWN A COMPUTERIZED SEWING MACHINE, THE DESIGN POSSIBILITIES ARE NEARLY ENDLESS. You can stitch entire scenes in thread, similar to designs found on antique crazy quilts. There is a wide variety of computer cards available that have whimsical motifs ideal for quiltmaking.

Even with a regular sewing machine that has only a few decorative stitches, you can enjoy crazy quilting. Have fun and LET YOUR IMAGINATION BE YOUR GUIDE!

Crazy Piecing

CRAZY PATCHWORK IS AN OLD QUILTING ART.
HERE, I INCORPORATE SOME CONTEMPORARY STRIP-PIECING
TECHNIQUES TO SPEED THE PROCESS.

GENERAL INSTRUCTIONS

1. Organize the fabric scraps.

• Collect fabric scraps of similar colors.

• Cut numerous polygon-shaped center sections (shown as white patches in the diagrams), each with sides approximately 2" to 3" (5 cm to 7.5 cm) as shown in *Diagram A*.

• Cut remaining scraps into strips of various widths.

2. Stitch crazy quilt blocks, using an adaptation of Log Cabin technique.

• Place a center section on one of the fabric strips, with the right sides together, aligning one edge of the center section along the strip. Repeat, placing additional center sections along the strip. Allow space between center sections to provide room for cutting the strip into separate sections.

• Stitch the center sections to the strip with a narrow seam allowance *(Diagram B)*. A ¼" (0.6 cm) seam allowance is traditional, but not essential. After all, this is crazy quilting!

• Open the fabric so that the right sides of both fabrics face up. Press or finger-press seam allowances in one direction.

• Cut the joined pieces apart.

• Place a second fabric strip on the bed of the sewing machine, with the right side up. Align the crazy pieces along one edge of that strip, with the right sides together, to determine spacing, again allowing extra fabric between sections for angle cuts. Stitch the strips together *(Diagram C)*. Open fabrics so

that the right sides face up. Press seam allowances in one direction.

• Cut sections, again following the angle of the crazy piece.

• Add subsequent strips so that the crazy piece forms a somewhat square shape. The shape will not be perfectly square; you will trim it to size once all of the piecing is done.

3. Decide on a uniform size for your crazy blocks, say, 6" to 8" (15 cm to

20.5 cm). Use a quilting ruler to trim all the crazy pieces to the desired size *(Diagram D)*.

> *Note from Nancy:* Use your creativity in cutting these squares. Not all of them have to be cut following the straight of grain; turn your ruler to cut some squares at an angle. Just go with your personal preference. Remember, you're the designer!

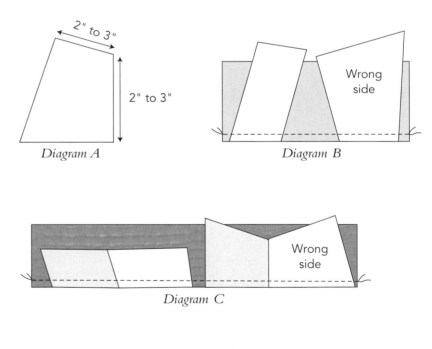

Diagram A

Diagram B

Diagram C

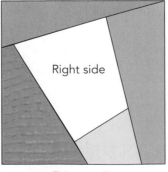

Diagram D

4. Stitch the squares together to create a patchwork piece. Back the squares with a piece of 100%-cotton muslin or flannel *(Diagram E)*.

5. Embellish the patchwork with decorative stitches.

• Select one or more decorative stitches. Stitch along seams of the crazy patchwork to embellish it *(Diagram F)*. This is an ideal project for a beginner. Just doodle at the machine!

• Randomly stitch along several seams of the crazy piecing. For best results, use rayon embroidery thread, a machine embroidery needle, and lightweight thread in the bobbin. Loosen the top tension by two numbers (or two notches).

• Change threads and/or patterns as desired.

6. After the decorative stitches are added to the crazy patchwork section, wash and dry the piece. The cotton backing usually shrinks slightly, creating a puckered look.

Flannel or muslin

Diagram E

Note from Nancy: I "floss" my tension disks whenever I change threads. Instead of pulling the old thread out from the thread spool, I clip the thread at the spool and pull the thread down and out through the machine needle. This helps clean lint from the tension disks and prevents lint buildup that might cause stitching problems.

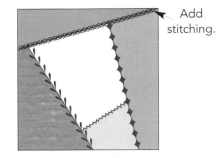

Add stitching.

Diagram F

Crazy Quilt

EXPERIMENT WITH YOUR COMPUTERIZED SEWING MACHINE. KEEP THE
SAMPLES YOU STITCH AND THEN USE THEM WITH YOUR SCRAP FABRICS TO
MAKE A FABULOUS CRAZY QUILT! OF COURSE, YOUR QUILT CENTERS DO NOT
HAVE TO BE COMPUTER-GENERATED—USE WHATEVER INSPIRES YOU.

**Quilt by Cindy Wilson
and Carol Wright**

MATERIALS

1½ yards (1.40 m) white fabric for
  block centers
⅜ yard (0.35 m) each (or scraps) of
  10 fabrics for crazy piecing
1½ yards (1.40 m) border fabric
1⅝ yards (1.60 m) fabric for backing
Twin-size batting
½ yard (0.50 m) fabric for binding
Machine-embroidery threads
Silk ribbon

CUTTING
🕐 30 Minutes 🕐

From the white fabric, cut:
• Five 10"-wide (25.5 cm-wide)
  strips. Cut each strip into four 10"
  (25.5 cm) squares for center motif.

From the assorted fabrics, cut:
• Three 4"-wide (10 cm-wide) strips
  from each.

From the border fabric:
• Choose the desired width of the
  borders, based on the print you use.
• Cut four lengthwise strips the border width plus ½" (1.3 cm) for the
  seam allowances.

From the binding fabric, cut:
• Seven 2¼"-wide (5.6 cm-wide)
  strips.

BLOCK ASSEMBLY
🕐 10–20 Minutes Each 🕐

1. Select designs for the block centers. Back the fabric with stabilizer
and machine-embroider the images.
As a substitute, use novelty prints, old
decorative handkerchiefs, or hand-
embroidered pieces in the center.
2. Referring to the general instructions on pages 100 and 101, trim the
center sections into polygon shapes
and sew assorted pieces to them
crazy-style.
3. Square up blocks to 8½" (21.8 cm).

QUILT ASSEMBLY
🕐 30 Minutes per Block 🕐

1. Sew over all the block seams with
decorative stitches, as detailed on
page 101.
2. Join blocks into five horizontal
rows of four blocks each. Join rows.
3. Add borders to the quilt in the
width you desire.

FINISHING

1. Layer backing (facedown), batting,
and quilt top (faceup).
2. Tie the quilt with silk ribbons at
block intersections.
3. Join 2¼"-wide (5.6 cm-wide)
strips into one piece for straight-grain
binding. Add the binding to the quilt.

GET THIS LOOK

Carol Wright used her computerized
Pfaff and the memory cards listed
below to make the block centers.
Frog: Amazing Design Embroidery
Design Pack AD 119, Frog
Collection I
Hat: Amazing Designs Pfaff Memory
Card PFMC 110, Country Garden
Collection I
Small Butterfly: Pfaff Memory
Card CF7560, Pattern #13
Medium Butterfly: Pfaff Choice
Memory Card, Nancy Zieman's
Favorite Designs #12
Large Butterfly: Pfaff Memory
Card #1, Pattern #1
Heart: Pfaff Memory Card #57,
Appliqué Pattern #16

Christmas Stocking

USE METALLIC THREAD, RICH HOLIDAY PRINTS, AND
DECORATIVE MACHINE STITCHES TO CREATE THIS ELEGANT STOCKING.

Stocking made by
Donna Fenske

MATERIALS

¾ yard (0.70 m) Fabric A for lining

½ yard (0.50 m) Fabric B for stocking cuff and crazy piecing

¼ yard (0.25m) Fabric C for crazy
piecing

CUTTING
 20 Minutes

1. Choose three coordinating cotton
fabrics. I chose a tone-on-tone print
(A), a striped fabric (B), and an allover print (C). Cut out the following
sections:

From Fabric A, cut:

- Three 12" x 18" (30.5 cm x 46
  cm) rectangles for the stocking
  back and the lining front and back.

- One 6½" x 12½" (16.3 cm x 31.8
  cm) rectangle for the stocking top
  section.

- Three 2"- or 2½"-wide (5 cm- or
  6.3 cm-wide) strips, each 15" (38
  cm) long, for the patchwork
  (*Diagram A*).

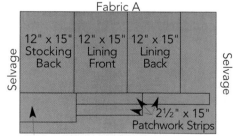

Diagram A

From Fabric B, cut:

- Two cuff sections, using enlarged
  pattern (page 107).

- Three 2"- or 2½"-wide (5 cm- or
  6.3 cm-wide) strips, each 15" (38
  cm) long, for the patchwork.

- One 1¾" x 9" (4.5 cm x 23 cm) strip for the hanging loop (Diagram B).

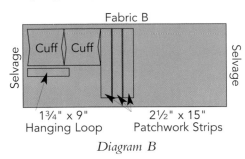

Diagram B

From Fabric C, cut:

- Three 2"- or 2½"-wide (5 cm- or 6.3 cm-wide) strips, each 15" (38cm) long, for the patchwork.

STOCKING ASSEMBLY
⏱ 30 Minutes ⏱

Note: All seam allowances are ¼" (0.6 cm) unless otherwise indicated.

2. Join the strips to create a pieced unit for the stocking front.

- Recut one edge of the Fabric A stocking top at an angle, so that the right side measures 4½" (11.5 cm) (Diagram C). This will be the top section of the stocking.

- Align one cut strip C along the angle cut of top section A, right sides together. Join fabrics (Diagram D). Fold strip so that right side faces up.

- Add seven or eight additional strips in the same way, alternating prints and forming a pieced unit large enough for the stocking pattern. Press all seam allowances in the same direction.

- Back the pieced fabric with an iron-on stabilizer, such as Totally Stable™ (Diagram E).

3. Using chalk, trace the stocking pattern onto the right side of the pieced unit (Diagram F).

4. Add decorative stitching along one side of each stitched seam, following the techniques detailed on page 101 (Diagram G).

- Test-stitch selections, thread colors, and stabilizers on fabric samples before stitching on the project. Adjust your sewing machine as necessary.

- Stitch to the left of the seam, starting and stopping the stitching outside the chalk marking. The heavy concentration of stitching sometimes draws in the fabric slightly, so starting and ending outside the pattern outline provides a safety net to ensure that the stitching extends to the edges of the finished stocking.

- Align the seam line with a spot on the presser foot to keep the stitching a uniform distance from the seam.

- Allow the fabric to feed automatically through the machine. The presser foot moves the fabric back and forth as you stitch the design. Your job is to gently guide the fabric so the seam line continuously follows the correct spot on the presser foot.

- After completing all stitching, remove the stabilizer (Diagram H). Hold your thumb over the stitches and tear away the stabilizer with the other hand to avoid putting any stress on the stitching. Remove any remaining stabilizer with tweezers. ⟶

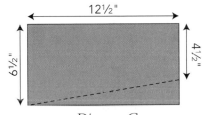

Diagram C

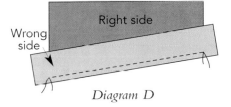

Diagram D

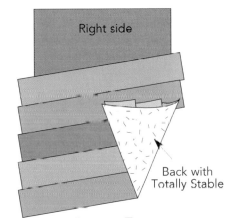

Diagram E

Diagram F

Diagram G

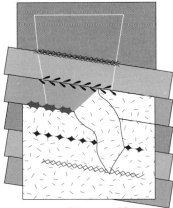

Diagram H

5. Stack the pieced unit and one of the 12" x 18" (30.5 cm x 46 cm) rectangles, with the wrong sides together. Cut out the stocking pattern along the drawn line *(Diagram I)*.

6. Join the stocking front and back, with the right sides together, stitching around the outer edges but leaving the top open *(Diagram J)*. Turn the stocking right side out.

7. Stack the remaining two Fabric A rectangles. Place the stocking pattern on top; cut out the lining. With the right sides facing and the raw edges aligned, stitch the outer edges, leaving the top open.

FINISHING
⏱ 30 Minutes ⏱

8. Add the cuff and the hanging loop.
• Insert the lining inside of the stocking, with the wrong sides together. Pin the top edges together, matching the seams *(Diagram K)*.
• Make a hanging loop.
  - Meet and join the lengthwise edges of the hanging loop, with the right sides together *(Diagram L)*. Stitch and turn right side out.
  - Fold the loop in half, meeting the cut edges. Place the loop inside the stocking, meeting the cut edges and centering the loop over the seam of the heel edge *(Diagram M)*.
• Add the cuff.
  - Join the angled ends of each cuff piece, with the right sides together *(Diagram N)*. Press the seam open.
  - Fold the cuff in half, with the wrong sides together, meeting the cut edges.
  - Place the cuff over the lining, meeting the cut edges. Stitch around the top of the stocking *(Diagram O)*.
  - Turn the cuff to the outside, covering the seam and pulling the hanging loop up; press.

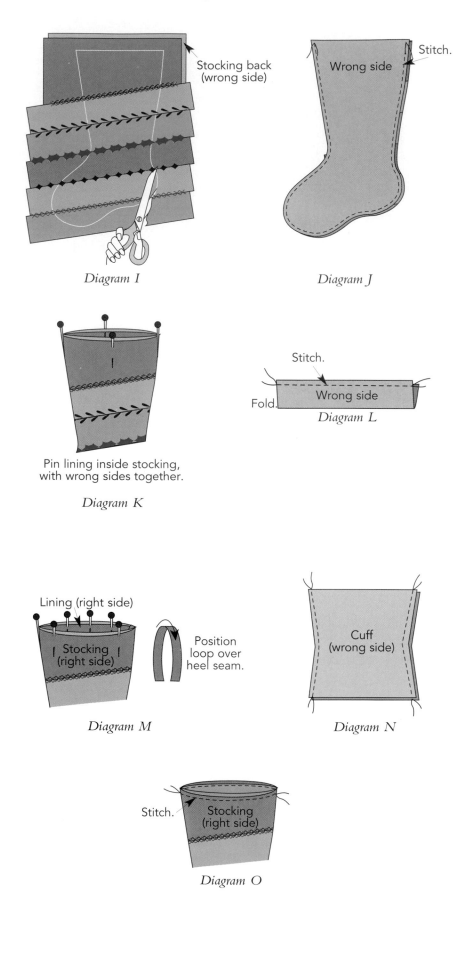

Diagram I

Diagram J

Pin lining inside stocking, with wrong sides together.

Diagram K

Diagram L

Diagram M

Diagram N

Diagram O

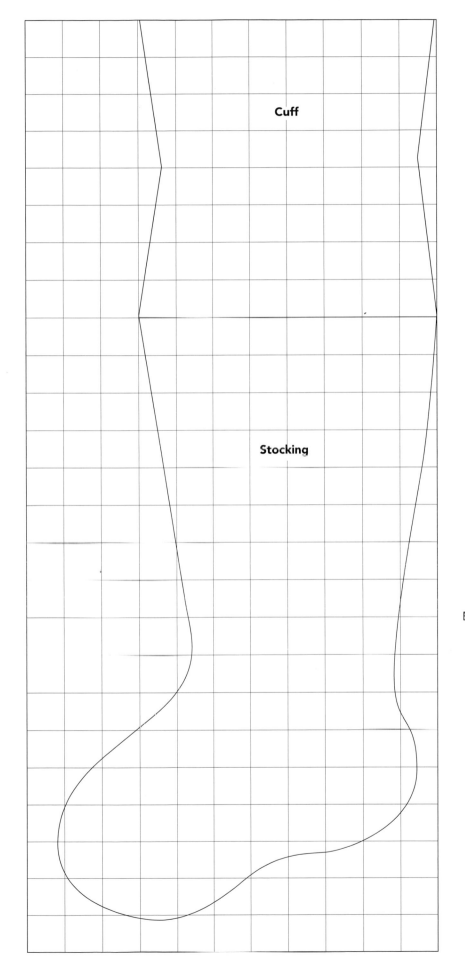

Cuff

Stocking

One square = 1".
Enlarge pattern 370% (or
129% and then another
200%).

8

Gifts to Go

Birthdays! Christmas! Mother's Day! Father's Day! Weddings! Anniversaries! IT SEEMS LIKE WE ARE CONSTANTLY SEARCHING FOR THE PERFECT GIFT FOR A SPECIAL OCCASION.

EACH OF US LIKES TO GIVE—AND TO RECEIVE—UNIQUE

HANDMADE GIFTS. But because of our busy schedules, we sometimes have little time to make those cherished gifts.

THIS CHAPTER OFFERS A SOLUTION. It includes instructions for making distinctive gifts that can be completed in only 10 to 30 minutes. So the next time you need a gift for someone special, try one of these super-quick and easy-to-sew projects.

Totables by
Nancy Zieman

10-Minute Totables

MY FIRST GIFT IDEA REQUIRES ONLY SCRAPS OF FABRIC AND FOUR ROWS OF MACHINE STITCHING. TOTABLES ARE GREAT FOR STORING SHOES, JEWELRY, LINGERIE, OR MANY OTHER ITEMS. TRAVELERS WILL FIND THESE ATTRACTIVE QUILTED BAGS INVALUABLE—AND THE TOTES ARE IDEAL FOR "WRAPPING" GIFTS, TOO.

MATERIALS

Note: This project takes 10 to 20 minutes if you work with prequilted fabric and use a ribbon for the handle. The examples shown at left were made from machine-pieced units and took about an hour each to make. See page 30 to make the Four-Patch pattern (left) or page 20 to make the Roman Stripe pattern (right) shown in the photo on the opposite page.

• **Fabric rectangle:** Quilted fabrics are ideal—or use two layers of non-quilted fabric.

  – 12" wide x 6" deep (30.5 cm wide x 15 cm deep) piece for small tote for jewelry or little gifts, as shown in *Diagram A*.

  – 18" wide x 12" deep (46 cm wide x 30.5 cm deep) piece for medium tote for lingerie or medium-sized items, as shown in *Diagram B*.

  – 24" wide x 18" deep (61 cm wide x 46 cm deep) piece for large tote for shoes or bigger items, as shown in *Diagram C*.

• **Zipper:** Use one at least 2" (5 cm) longer than the depth of the tote. A longer zipper allows the pull tab to extend beyond the tote when the zipper is inserted; you won't have to contend with the zipper pull during stitching, since it can be pulled out of the way.

• **Ribbon:** Purchase either grosgrain or satin ribbon, about 6" (15 cm) long for the handle. Or make a fabric handle by sewing two 2½" x 6" (6.3 cm

x 15 cm) fabric pieces together, with right sides facing, and then turning them right side out. Machine-quilt the handle in a grid, if desired. You may also use a piece of prepackaged bias tape.

ASSEMBLY

1. Secure the handle to the bag.
• Find the center of the rectangle by folding it in half, meeting the two

shorter edges. Mark the center with a pin *(Diagram D)*.
• Fold the handle in half, meeting the cut edges. Place the handle fold at the marked center of the rectangle, aligning the cut edges of the ribbon with the cut edges of the fabric and allowing the folded edge of the handle to extend onto the fabric. Machine-baste the handle in place *(Diagram E)*. ⟶

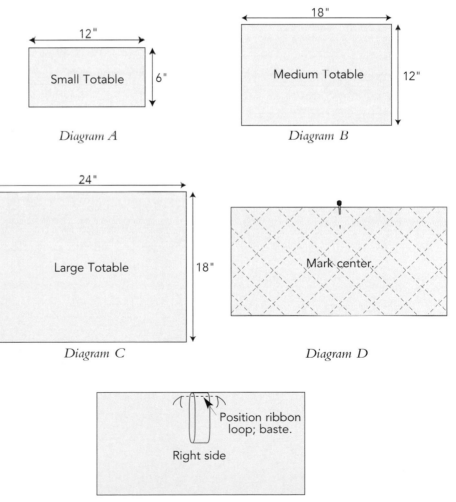

12"

Small Totable   6"

Diagram A

18"

Medium Totable   12"

Diagram B

24"

Large Totable   18"

Diagram C

Mark center.

Diagram D

Position ribbon loop; baste.

Right side

Diagram E

2. Insert the zipper.

• Press under ½" to ⅝" (1.3 cm to 1.5 cm) seam allowances on the short edges of the rectangle.

• Position one of the folded edges along one side of the zipper teeth, with the zipper facing up and the tab extending above the seam.

• Topstitch the fold to the zipper, sewing from the right side of the fabric *(Diagram F).*

• Stitch the remaining seam allowance to the other side of the zipper teeth *(Diagram G).*

• Pull the zipper tab down to the middle of the bag.

3. Stitch the upper edge of the tote.

• Turn the tote wrong side out.

• Position the zipper so that the center of the tote meets the center of the zipper.

• Stitch or serge, reinforcing the stitching at the zipper intersection *(Diagram H).*

4. Stitch the lower edge of the tote.

• Refold the tote so that the center of the zipper is aligned at one side.

• Stitch or serge, reinforcing the stitching at the zipper intersection *(Diagram I).*

• Turn the tote right side out *(Diagram J).*

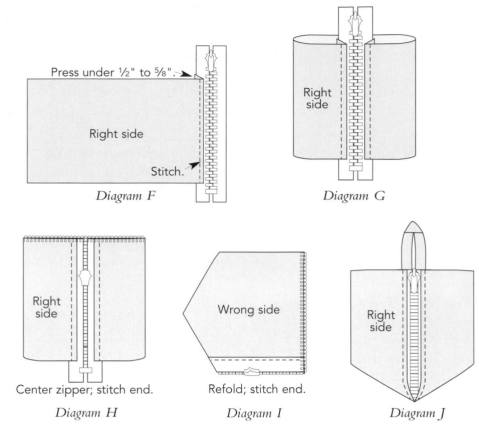

Press under ½" to ⅝".

Right side

Stitch.

Diagram F

Right side

Diagram G

Right side

Center zipper; stitch end.

Diagram H

Wrong side

Refold; stitch end.

Diagram I

Right side

Diagram J

MORE IDEAS

 If you or a friend enjoy taking quilt classes, make these totables to carry your quilting supplies. Consider stitching one to store your iron and one to store general supplies, such as a rotary cutter, scissors, and other small notions.

Often, you can find designer fabric remnants at a significant discount at a retail fabric store or an interior decorator's shop. Use these pieces to make elegant totes for friends to use when they travel.

Save bias tape pieces left over from other projects. Use these snippets to make handles for totables.

Stitch some totables in prequilted Christmas prints, which are widely available in retail fabric stores during the holidays. Tuck a gift inside each, making the totable not only the wrapping, but also an extra gift in itself!

Nancy's Mailbag

MY VIEWERS AND MAIL-ORDER CUSTOMERS HAVE A WEALTH
OF QUILTING INFORMATION. I ENJOY READING YOUR
LETTERS AND SHARING YOUR FAVORITE TIPS AND TECHNIQUES.
BELOW ARE JUST A FEW HELPFUL QUILTING TIPS.

I made a small pillow from some of my late husband's neckties. The ties were too nice to discard, so I combined pieces of the fabrics to create a remembrance. I made seven pillows for family members.

G.L., McGregor, Iowa

I purchase extra-long manicure sticks from a beauty-supply store. (You might be able to obtain one from your beautician.) I find these sticks most helpful in easing fabric under the needle. The sticks are very lightweight, and the 6" (15 cm) length is a comfortable size to handle.

D.B., Edneyville, North Carolina

I had been frustrated with digging through a drawer for a spool of the right color thread. As I was sorting through some items, I discovered a spice rack from my kitchen. I didn't want to throw it away, so I decided to use it in my sewing room. I hung it on the wall next to my sewing machine and put the spools of thread on it.

E.W., Norwalk, California

VISIT OUR WEB SITE:

WWW.SEWINGWITHNANCY.COM

• Get updates on *Sewing With Nancy®* programs.
• Receive our free E-mail newsletter.
• Contact our knowledgeable sewing advisors.
• Shop the on-line catalog.
• Look for exclusive on-line products.

Cat by Shelby
Sawyer Morris

Nine-Patch Cat

ALONG WITH HIS NINE LIVES, THIS CAT HAS NINE
PATCHES! THIS SMALL PROJECT USES UP SCRAPS OF FABRIC
TO MAKE A "PURR-FECT" GIFT FOR A FRIEND.

MATERIALS

Nine 4" (10 cm) assorted squares
8" x 12" (20.5 cm x 30. 5 cm) piece
  of fabric for backing
Polyester fiberfill

BLOCK ASSEMBLY
🕐 10 Minutes 🕐

1. Arrange squares to form a Nine-Patch block. See how the colors and the fabrics will look in the finished project *(Diagram A)*.
2. Stack Rows 1 and 2 *(Diagram B)*, with right sides facing, and chain-piece, using a ¼" (0.6 cm) seam allowance *(Diagram C)*. **Do not** clip

the threads at the end of each seam; butt the next set of squares to the previous set and continue stitching.
3. Sew Row 3 to Rows 1 and 2, repeating the chain-piecing technique.
4. Press the seam allowances of the first and third stitched rows to the right. Press the seam allowances of the second row to the left. Clip threads between the strips *(Diagram D)*.
5. Join the top and center strips, with the right sides together and the edges even. Press the seam allowances toward the top. Stitch the lower strip to the other edge of the center strip; press the seams toward the top, forming a Nine-Patch block.

ASSEMBLY
🕐 30 Minutes 🕐

1. Stack a Nine-Patch block on top of the backing fabric, with the wrong sides together.
2. Trace the cat pattern (page 116). Position the pattern over the Nine-Patch and cut out.
3. Stitch right sides together with a ¼" (0.6 cm) seam allowance, leaving a 2" (5 cm) opening for stuffing.
4. Turn the cat right side out and stuff. Stitch the opening closed. Add face details with a permanent fabric marker or embroidery floss. ⟶

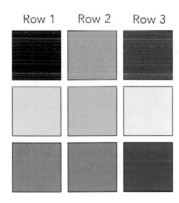

Row 1   Row 2   Row 3

Diagram A

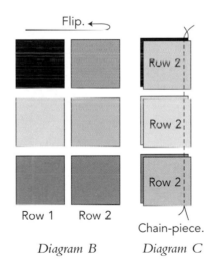

Flip. ⟵

Row 1   Row 2

Row 2

Row 2

Row 2

Chain-piece.

Diagram B   *Diagram C*

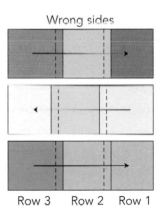

Wrong sides

Row 3   Row 2   Row 1

Diagram D

Cat

Comfort Pillow

IF YOU HAVE A STIFF NECK, AN ACHING KNEE, OR A SORE BACK, YOU'LL FIND SOOTHING RELIEF WITH THIS PILLOW. FILL IT WITH UNCOOKED RICE, BUCKWHEAT HULLS, CHERRY PITS, OR DRIED FIELD CORN. THEN HEAT IT IN THE MICROWAVE TO PROVIDE WARMTH AND RELIEF.

Comfort pillow by
Shelby Sawyer Morris

MATERIALS

½ yard (0.50 m) cotton print fabric

Coordinating scraps for quilt block

¼ yard (0.25 m) fabric for frame

Two 8" x 9" (20.5 cm x 23 cm) pieces cotton batting

2 pounds of uncooked rice, buckwheat hulls, cherry pits, or dried field corn

¼ yard fabric stabilizer

BLOCK ASSEMBLY
⏱ 20 Minutes Each ⏱

From a light scrap, cut:

• Two 2" (5 cm) squares for block centers.

• Four 2⅜" (6 cm) squares. Cut each square in half diagonally to make eight corner triangles.

• Eight 1¼" x 2" (3.2 cm x 5 cm) pieces for frame.

From a dark scrap, cut:

• Four 2⅜" (6 cm) squares. Cut each square in half diagonally to make eight corner triangles.

• Eight 1¼" x 2" (3.2 cm x 5 cm) pieces for frame.

1. Join the light triangles and the dark triangles along the bias edges to make eight corner squares. Press the seam toward the dark fabric.

2. Join the light rectangles to the dark rectangles. Press toward the dark fabric.

3. Arrange the pieces as shown in the *Block Assembly Diagram*. Join the pieces into rows. Join the rows to complete the quilt block *(Block Diagram)*.

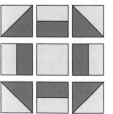

Block Assembly Diagram

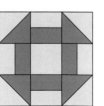

Block Diagram

COMFORT PILLOW ASSEMBLY
⏱ 30 Minutes ⏱

1. Make a pattern.

• Cut one 8" x 18" (20.5 cm x 46 cm) rectangle of paper.

• Fold the paper in half, meeting lengthwise edges.

• Place the 45° line of a quilting ruler along the fold, starting at one end. Mark along the edge of the ruler; cut along the traced line *(Diagram A)*.

• Open the paper pattern. Write "Place on fold" along the straight short end of the pattern.

2. Fold the fabric, meeting the selvages. Place the pattern on the fabric, aligning fold lines. Cut two pieces from the fabric *(Diagram B)*.

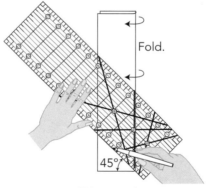

Diagram A

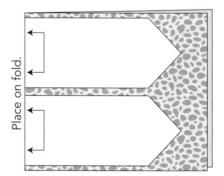

Diagram B

3. Appliqué the quilt blocks to both ends of one of the print fabric sections.

• Cut two 5" (12.5 cm) squares of frame fabric to highlight the quilt blocks.

• Position the frames behind the blocks as shown in *Diagram C*; pin in place. Place framed squares on opposite ends of one of the pillow pieces, with the right sides up. Pin and then straight-stitch close to outer edges to secure the squares for satin stitching.

• Satin-stitch the squares in place.

  - Back the fabric with stabilizer.

  - Set the machine for a satin stitch with a 0.5 length and a 2.0 width.

  - Satin-stitch around the framed sections. Change threads and satin-stitch around the quilt block *(Diagram D)*.

  - Remove excess stabilizer.

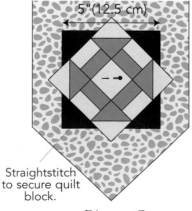

Straightstitch to secure quilt block.

Diagram C

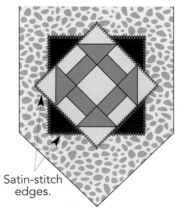

Satin-stitch edges.

Diagram D

⏱ 30 Minutes ⏱

4. Construct the pillow.

• Meet the fabric sections, with the right sides together. Place a piece of cotton batting at each end of the pillow; trim to fit the pillow.

• Stitch a ¼" (0.6 cm) seam along one edge of the pillow *(Diagram E)*. Trim the batting close to the stitching line. Press the seam flat; then fold the seam along the stitching line toward the center of the pillow.

• Stitch the adjacent edge of the pillow, beginning at the fold and sewing to the next edge, as shown in *Diagram F*. (This is a wrapped corner.) Trim the batting and press the seam as for the first edge.

• Repeat, wrapping corners on remaining sides, leaving a 4" to 6" (10 cm to 15 cm) opening along the final lengthwise edge *(Diagram G)*.

• Turn the pillow right side out. Press.

• Straightstitch around the blocks through all layers, extending stitching to the edges of the pillow at sides *(Diagram H)*. This will prevent the filling from settling in the ends and allow more filling in the neck area. However, if you want the filling to move freely inside, do not extend the stitching to the edges and add about 1 pound more of the filling.

• Fill the pillow with 2 pounds of rice, buckwheat hulls, cherry pits, or dried field corn. Stitch the opening closed.

5. To use the pillow, heat it in the microwave for 2 minutes. Move the filling inside the pillow from side to side to distribute the heat; then place the pillow on your body wherever you want soothing heat.

Diagram E

Diagram F

Diagram G

Diagram H

Nancy's Mailbag

I purchased a thimble with a recessed end, cut a magnet circle to fit the end, and glued the magnet in place. When I want to pick up a needle, I just hold my thimble over it. It's great!

K.O., Memphis, Tennessee

I find that when machine quilting in-the-ditch, I need to gently ease the two fabric sections apart to keep from catching fabric edges in the stitching. Because I work with cotton fabrics, I find it difficult to get a good grip on the fabrics to ease them apart. My tip is to buy rubber fingers, normally used for turning pages more easily, at office supply stores. I place them on the fingers I use to ease the fabrics apart.

H.M., Calgary, Alberta, Canada

Carrier by Kate Bashynski

Casserole Carrier

COMBINE NINE-PATCH AND SNOWBALL BLOCKS TO MAKE THIS INSULATING CASSEROLE WRAP. THIS QUILTED CARRIER, SUITABLE FOR SQUARE OR SMALL RECTANGULAR CASSEROLES, WILL KEEP HOT FOODS HOT AND COLD FOODS COLD.

Finished Size: About 23" x 23" (58.5 cm x 58.5 cm).

MATERIALS

⅞ yard (0.80 m) Fabric A (print) for Nine-Patch blocks and backing

⅓ yard (0.32 m) Fabric B (medium solid) for Snowball blocks and Nine-Patch mitts

½ yard (0.50 m) Fabric C (light solid) for Nine-Patch blocks and Snowball blocks

Two 23" (58.5 cm) squares of both batting and "Iron Quick" Teflon™ Coated Fabric

Two 8" (20.5 cm) squares of "Iron Quick" Teflon-Coated Fabric for pockets

Four 8" (20.5 cm) squares of batting for pockets

2 yards (1.85 m) of bias tape made from 2" (5 cm) strips (A 15" [38 cm] square provides sufficient fabric.)

CUTTING
⏱ 30 Minutes ⏱

From Fabric A, cut:

• Two 3" x 44" (7.5 cm x 112 cm) strips for Nine-Patch blocks.

• One 3" x 21" (7.5 cm x 53.5 cm) strip for Nine-Patch blocks.

• One 23" (58.5 cm) square.

• 2½"-wide (6.3 cm-wide) strips for binding.

From Fabric B, cut:

• Four 8" (20.5 cm) Snowball squares.

• Two 3" x 12" (7.5 cm x 30.5 cm) strips for mitt Nine-Patch blocks.

• Two 2" x 44" (5 cm x 112 cm) strips for mitt binding.

From Fabric C, cut:

• One 3" x 44" (7.5 cm x 112 cm) strip for Nine-Patch blocks.

• Two 3" x 21" (7.5 cm x 53.5 cm) strips for Nine-Patch blocks.

• One 3" x 12" (7.5 cm x 30.5 cm) strip for Mitt Nine-Patch blocks.

• Sixteen 3" (7.5 cm) squares for Snowball corners.

• Two 8" (20.5 cm) squares for mitt backings.

BLOCK ASSEMBLY
⏱ 30 Minutes ⏱

1. Make seven Nine-Patch blocks. (Use 3" [7.5 cm] strips, following the technique detailed on page 115.) Set two blocks aside.

2. Make four Snowball blocks.

• Choose one 8" (20.5 cm) block and four 3" (7.5 cm) squares.

• Referring to *Diagonal Seams Diagrams*, place one 3" (7.5 cm) square atop one corner of the 8" (20.5 cm) square. Stitch diagonally from corner to corner as shown. Trim ¼" (0.6 cm) from sewing line and press open. Repeat on the opposite diagonal corner.

• Repeat on the remaining corners to complete one Snowball block.

• Make four Snowball blocks for the Casserole Carrier. →

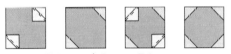

Diagonal Seams Diagrams

Fabric A Cutting Diagram

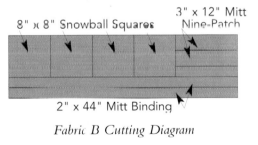

Fabric B Cutting Diagram

Fabric C Cutting Diagram

CARRIER ASSEMBLY
⏱ 30 Minutes ⏱

1. Referring to pages 16 and 17 for working with strip sets, stitch five Nine-Patch blocks and four Snowball blocks together as shown in *Diagram A* to form a 23" (58.5 cm) square. This will be the exterior of the quilt sandwich.

2. For the top, create a quilt "sandwich" including the pieced top.
• Place a layer of batting and a layer of "Iron Quick" fabric behind the patchwork square, with the shiny side of the "Iron Quick" exposed. Pin the layers together *(Diagram B)*.
• Stitch all the layers together, stitching in-the-ditch through the patchwork seams *(Diagram C)*.

3. Create the bottom by placing the second layer of batting next to the wrong side of the backing fabric *(Diagram D)*. With the batting next to the feed dogs, stitch layers together, using a 2½" (6.3 cm) grid. Set aside for use in Step 5.

Note from Nancy: For a fast and accurate way of marking a gridded quilting design on the backing fabric, use the Grid Maker™. Line up the edge of your quilt with the desired line or angle marking. Then use your favorite marking tool to draw your quilting lines, repositioning the Grid Marker as needed. After drawing the first set of lines, line up the adjacent edge of the quilt with the desired line or angle marking and draw the intersecting quilting lines.

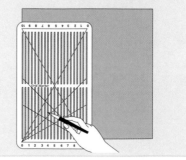

4. Make two mitt/spoon pockets.
• Create a quilt sandwich, layering in the following order: a Nine-Patch, an 8" (20.5 cm) batting square, an 8"-square (20.5 cm-square) piece of Teflon-coated fabric (with the shiny side facing the backing), a second layer of batting, and the backing *(Diagram E)*
• Stitch all the layers together, stitching in-the-ditch through the patchwork seams *(Diagram F)*.

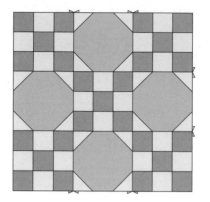
Diagram A

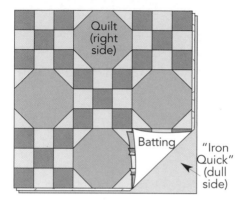
Diagram B

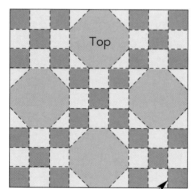
Stitch in-the-ditch.
Diagram C

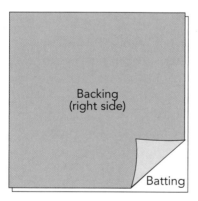
Diagram D

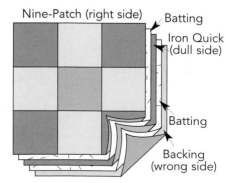
Diagram E

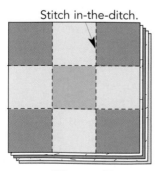
Diagram F

- Bind the edges (*Diagram G*).
- Repeat to make a second mitt/spoon pocket.
- Optional: Stitch a diagonal buttonhole in the outer corner of each mitt, sewing only through the mitt *(Diagram H)*. Sew corresponding buttons on the backing fabric, underneath the buttonhole. This allows you to button the pocket shut.
- Place a mitt on the right side of the backing fabric, approximately 1" to 1½" (2.5 cm to 3.8 cm) from the adjacent edges. Repeat, placing the second mitt at the opposite corner *(Diagram I)*.
- Stitch the inner two sides of each mitt to the backing fabric to create pockets *(Diagram J)*.
5. Stack the two quilted pieces with the unpieced side of the top facing the batting side of the bottom. Machine-baste the edges together.
6. Bind the edges with bias binding.
7. Stitch the buttonholes and the buttons.
- Stitch diagonal buttonholes at each corner as shown in *Diagram K*.

Note from Nancy: Because the buttonholes are going through multiple layers, you may want to use a slightly longer stitch length. And for added durability, cord the buttonholes or double-stitch them.

- String two buttons together, with the wrong sides together. The string should make the buttons about 1" (2.5 cm) apart. Insert one button through one buttonhole *(Diagram L)*.
- When you fold the carrier corners together over the casserole, insert the bottom button through the remaining three buttonholes to secure the cover.

Diagram G

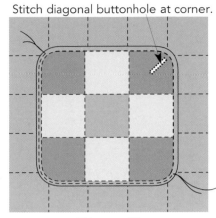

Stitch diagonal buttonhole at corner.

Diagram H

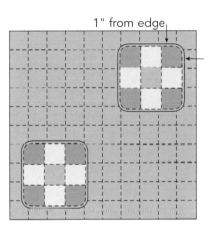

1" from edge

Diagram I

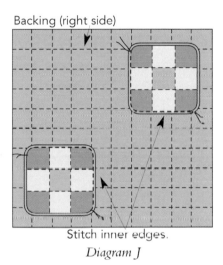

Backing (right side)

Stitch inner edges.

Diagram J

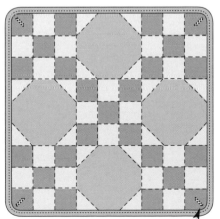

Stitch diagonal buttonholes
at each corner.

Diagram K

Diagram L

9

Machine Quilting

Machine quilting is a fast and easy way to join the layers of a quilted project, but there's more to machine quilting than merely sewing the layers together. THE ROAD TO QUICK QUILTING IS PAVED WITH TIMESAVING NOTIONS AND UPDATED TECHNIQUES. In this chapter, you'll find a collection of ideas that will simplify machine quilting techniques.

Start by creating a quilt "sandwich" with a special pinning process. After assembling the sandwich, join the layers by stitching in-the-ditch, which is a quick machine-quilting technique.

EXPERIMENT WITH OTHER STITCHING OPTIONS, including diagonal stitching, geometric motifs, or more detailed designs. Then join quilt sections with a simple quilt-as-you-go technique. Finally, learn to use press-on templates to add continuous scallop quilting to a quilt project.

These tried-and-true methods will speed your quilting, plus give it special flair and dimension. Enjoy!

Creating the Quilt Sandwich

MOST QUILTS INCLUDE THREE LAYERS: THE QUILT TOP,
THE BATTING, AND THE BACKING. PREPARING THOSE LAYERS FOR
QUILTING IS THE FIRST STEP IN THE QUILTING PROCESS.

LAYERING THE QUILT

Top Layer

1. Fabrics of 100% cotton are traditionally used for quilt tops.

2. Here are several options for preparing the quilt top.

• Choose a printed quilt panel.

• Use a piece of solid colored fabric.

• Piece several fabrics to prepare the quilt top. To determine how to press the pieced seams, decide how the quilt will be machine-quilted.

 - If stitching in-the-ditch, press the seams open to make it easier to stitch in-the-ditch *(Diagram A)*.

 - If stitching across seams or avoiding them entirely, press the seams to one side *(Diagram B)*.

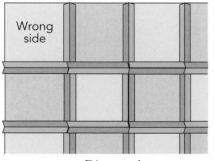

Diagram A

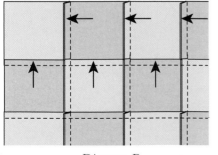

Diagram B

Batting Layer

1. Batting is available in several fiber contents and weights.

• Cotton and cotton-blend batts

 - Cotton batts are lightweight and soft, and they drape well.

 - Cotton batts have low loft (thickness).

 - Cotton battings are easy to quilt by machine, making them a good choice for beginners.

• Polyester batts

 - Polyester batts are available in several different weights and are often listed by the number of ounces per yard. Use a batt with a weight no heavier than 10 ounces for machine quilting. Heavier weights are suited for hand tying but are too thick for machine quilting.

 - Polyester batts have greater loft than cotton, so quilts will be puffy.

 - Note the surface of the batt. Unless the surface is treated in some way, fibers can beard or work their way to the surface of the quilted project. Some batts are thermal bonded to prevent bearding; heat melts a portion of the fibers to serve as a natural bonding. Others have a scrim, which is a cloth backing attached to both sides to prevent fibers from migrating to the surface.

• Wool

 - Wool batts are warm, light, and wonderful to touch. They drape well and are easy to machine quilt.

 - Wool batts generally cost more than other batts.

2. The thicker the batting, the more difficult it is to quilt by machine.

3. The type of batt selected determines the distance between the rows of machine quilting.

• Batts of natural (cotton and wool) fibers need to be quilted more closely together than those of synthetic (polyester) fibers.

• Cotton and wool batts should be quilted every 1" to 2" (2.5 cm to 5 cm).

• Polyester batts should be quilted every 4" to 6" (10 cm to 15 cm).

Backing Layer

1. Use the same quality fabric as for the top layer. If the top layer is 100% cotton, choose a backing of 100% cotton.

2. To save time, consider using super-sized muslin (90" to 120" [229 cm to 305 cm]). The larger size usually eliminates the need to piece the quilt backing.

Note from Nancy: Using a basting gun or basting with safety pins is so much faster than traditional thread basting.

SECURING THE LAYERS

Try this two-step process to secure the three quilt layers. It's definitely easier than trying to work with all three layers at the same time.

1. Join the top and the batting.

• Place the batting on a flat surface, such as a tabletop or the floor. The batting should not extend over the sides of the table. (See the Quilter's Basting Grate on page 11.)

• Layer the quilt top and the batting, with wrong sides facing *(Diagram C)*.

• Pin the layers together with long straight pins, starting at the center and working outward. Pin periodically in a few key areas; this is a temporary pinning step *(Diagram D)*.

• Gently roll the fabric and set aside the pinned layers *(Diagram E)*.

2. Add the backing.

• Cut the backing at least 3" (7.5 cm) larger on each side than the quilt top, following the fabric grain.

• Place the backing fabric on a flat surface with the right side down.

• Tape all four edges of the fabric to the surface with masking tape to prevent shifting. This keeps the backing flat so that it does not stretch *(Diagram F)*.

• Layer the top/batting layer on the backing fabric. Pin the layers together with Curved Safety Pins or a Quilter's Basting Gun.

  - Curved Safety Pins have just the right angle for easy, comfortable insertion. Use size 1 pins when working with low-loft projects.

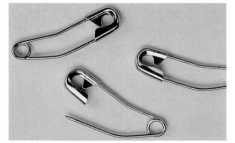

- A Quilter's Basting Gun temporarily staples layers together with extra-long (1 cm) plastic tacks *(Diagram G)*. When the quilting is finished, snip the tacks away. Put your hand under the fabric to lift it from the table or the floor as you baste, unless you work with a Quilter's Basting Grate (page 11).

• Remove the straight pins after the entire quilt top has been safely pinned or basted.

3. After securing the three layers, release the masking tape and roll one edge of the quilt to the center. Secure the roll with quilt clips, such as Jaws™. Repeat, rolling the opposite edge toward the center, leaving space in the middle for the quilting area *(Diagram H)*.   ⟶

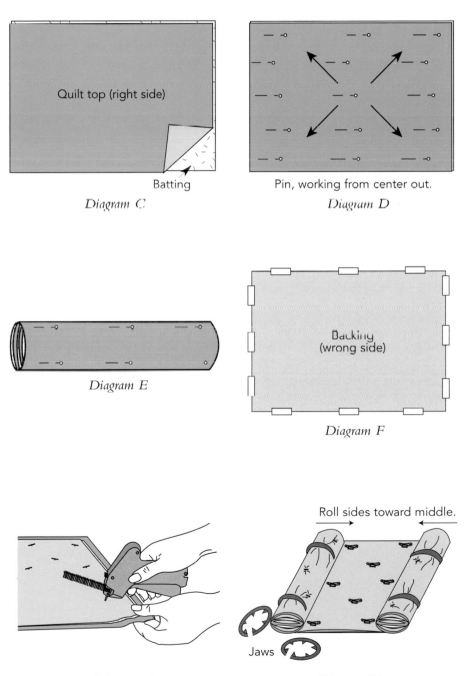

Quilt top (right side)

Batting

Diagram C

Pin, working from center out.

Diagram D

Diagram E

Backing (wrong side)

Diagram F

Roll sides toward middle.

Jaws

Diagram G

Diagram H

SEWING MACHINE SETUP

1. It's important to prevent the layers of the quilt sandwich from shifting. If your machine has dual feed, engage it to help the three layers feed evenly through the machine. If your machine does not have that capability, replace the conventional presser foot with a walking foot to move the quilt layers evenly through the machine *(Diagram I)*. This is the key element in machine quilting.

2. Optional: If your machine has dual feed, replace the conventional presser foot with an open toe or appliqué foot, if possible. Both have an open section in the center of the foot, providing greater visibility as you stitch *(Diagram J)*.

3. Insert a machine-quilting needle. These needles have a special taper to the point that helps sew through the thick layers of crossed seams in a quilted or patchwork project.

4. Fill the bobbin with 100%-cotton thread, matched to the backing fabric.

5. Thread the top of the machine with a monofilament thread, such as Madeira Monofil. Use clear Monofil for light fabrics and the smoke color for dark fabrics. Or use matching cotton thread or cotton/polyester thread.

6. Adjust the machine for a straight stitch.

7. If possible, adjust the machine to stop with the needle in the down position.

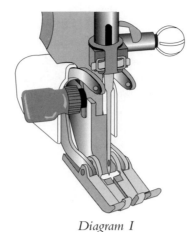

Diagram I

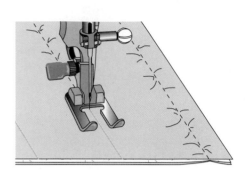

Diagram J

Nancy's Mailbag

I found myself in a very frustrating predicament recently. I had changed from a walking foot to a standard presser foot for my sewing machine and had to readjust the bobbin and thread tensions in the process. Unable to determine which thread was at fault, I spent an enormous amount of time trying to work out this simple problem. I was about ready to quit when I thought of using different colored threads for the bobbin and needle. I put a red thread through the needle and a yellow thread in the bobbin. This enabled me to adjust the tension easily and efficiently.

G.K., Palm Beach Gardens, Florida

After I have all my pieces cut for a quilting square, I place a bath towel on my cutting table and arrange the pieces in the pattern I've chosen. If necessary, I layer several towels in the same fashion. Then I simply roll up the towels and carry them to the sewing machine, carefully unrolling them on the sewing table. I can also tidy up quickly and put the strips away until later if my time is limited or my sewing is interrupted.

G.J., Pittsburgh, Pennsylvania

When I make a quilt, I prepare a chart of the fabric swatches. I place the chart and fabric scraps in a zip-top bag for possible future repairs. If I give the quilt as a gift, I include the zip-top bag.

M.M., North Fort Myers, Florida

Machine-Quilting the Quilt Sandwich

NOW THAT THE THREE QUILT LAYERS ARE SECURED AND THE MACHINE IS READY, IT'S TIME TO QUILT. STITCHING IN-THE-DITCH IS A GREAT MACHINE-QUILTING OPTION FOR PIECED QUILTS. OR TO ACHIEVE UNIFORM OVERALL MACHINE QUILTING, TRY THE DIAGONAL QUILTING VARIATION.

IN-THE-DITCH QUILTING

1. Begin in the center of the project.

2. Lock the threads.

• Set the stitch length to "0." Draw up the bobbin thread *(Diagram A)*. Sew in place two or three stitches to lock the threads; then clip the thread tails.

• Reset the stitch length to the normal length.

3. Stitch in-the-ditch along the quilt seams.

• Position your hands to the left and to the right of the needle. Use your hands to hold the fabric flat.

• Stitch in the well of the seam until you reach the end of the seam, gently pulling the fabric away from the needle area to make it easier to stitch in-the-ditch *(Diagram B)*. Move the safety pins safely out of the way as you sew.

• At the end of the seam, stop with the needle in the down position and lock the threads by returning the stitch length to "0" and sewing in place 3 to 4 stitches.

• Advance to the next section. (It's not necessary to clip threads at this point. To save time, clip thread tails after all the stitching is completed.) Reposition the fabric so that the quilt remains smooth and flat. Lock the threads and sew along that seam. Remember, space rows of stitching 1" to 2" (2.5 cm to

5 cm) apart with natural fiber batts and 4" to 6" (10 cm to 15 cm) apart with polyester batts *(Diagram C)*.

• Stitch additional rows until the entire quilt is quilted. Reroll and reclip the quilt as necessary.

4. After completing all the stitching, clip and remove the thread tails between the stitched sections *(Diagram D)*. →

> *Note from Nancy:* Stitching the center of the quilt is the most difficult part of the machine-quilting process because of all the excess bulk that will be to your left and right. Take your time so that the fabric is properly positioned. As you move toward the quilt's outer edges, it becomes easier to manipulate the fabric.

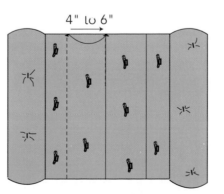

Diagram A

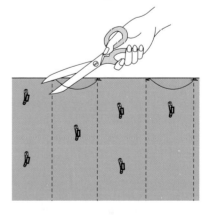

Diagram B

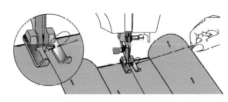

4" to 6"

Diagram C

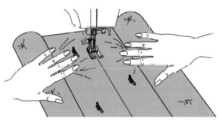

Diagram D

DIAGONAL MACHINE QUILTING

The beauty of this diagonal quilting technique, developed by Ernest Haight, is that except when stitching two long diagonal lines, the majority of the fabric is always to the left of the machine as you stitch, rather than in the bed of the machine.

Marking the quilt top is the most time-consuming part of this process, but it is the key to achieving precisely shaped and positioned stitching.

1. Mark the edges of the quilt top before pinning the layers together.

• Start at the upper left corner. Depending on whether the batt is a polyester or natural fiber, mark every 2" to 4" (5 cm to 10 cm) along the top edge *(Diagram E)*.

• Distances between the marks should be uniform, with the final mark at the upper right corner.

• Mark along the lower edge, following the same procedure. These markings should be parallel to those on the top row *(Diagram F)*.

• Mark the two side edges, again starting and stopping exactly at the corners *(Diagram G)*.

2. Mark the diagonal grids between the outer markings.

• Use a carpenter's chalk plumb line to mark the fabric. Or run chalk along a string and use that to transfer the lines. Or use a ruler and a chalk marker.

• If possible, enlist the help of a friend when you do this marking, as this will make it easier to transfer accurate lines.

• Begin at the upper right corner. Place the chalked string between the first mark on the top and the first mark on the side *(Diagram H)*. Hold the string taut; snap the string by lifting it at the center and releasing it. The chalk leaves a mark on the fabric that serves as a stitching guide.

• Move the string to the next set of markings; hold the string taut and snap *(Diagram I)*. The second line will be parallel to the first one. Repeat, marking all diagonal lines in one direction.

• Next, rotate the quilt and mark diagonal lines between the markings on the opposite top and side edges. Repeat until all the lines are marked, creating diamond shapes *(Diagram J)*.

3. Pin the backing (facedown), the batting, and the quilt top (faceup) together as detailed on page 127.

4. Stitch the layers together.

• Begin stitching at the upper left corner. Stitch across the quilt, following the marked lines, smoothing the fabric on each side of the presser foot with your hands as you sew.

• At the end of the marked line, where it intersects with another line, stop with the needle in the down position. Raise the presser foot; pivot the fabric 90°.

2" to 4"   2" to 4"

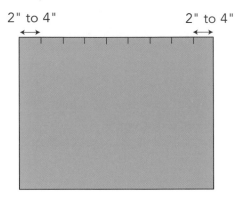

Diagram E

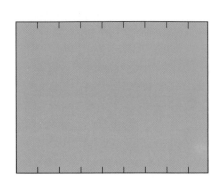

Diagram F

Diagram G

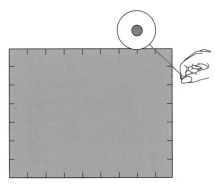

Diagram H

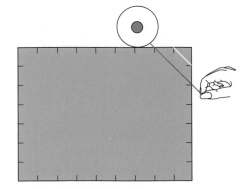

Diagram I

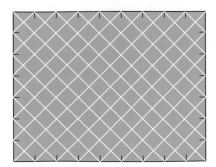

Diagram J

• Lower the presser foot and continue stitching. Move the safety pins out of the way as you come to them *(Diagram K)*.

• Repeat, pivoting and stitching.

• Continue until you run out of stitching lines.

• Rotate the quilt so that the unstitched lines are aligned at the upper left. Continue pivoting and stitching as detailed above *(Diagram L)*.

• After stitching the first two series of lines, begin again at the first upper left corner, moving one row to the right or the left. Repeat the sequence.

• Continue until all the lines have been stitched.

Start.

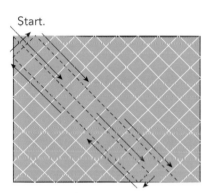

Diagram K

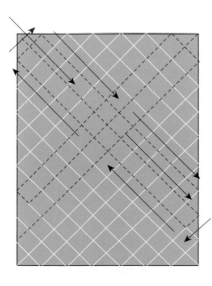

Diagram L

Nancy's Mailbag

I had a problem keeping my quilt strips organized when I quilted. I had strips of fabric lying all over the table, daybed, etc. To remedy this, I took hangers and clothespins and organized the strips into the fabrics I needed for each quilt. Now all I have to do is reach into the closet for the proper hanger to have all the strips at hand.

P.B., Port Richey, Florida

My mother-in-law gave me this tip. She is 94 years old and still makes beautiful quilts. She has trouble threading her needles and will have one of us do it for her. She has us thread 10 or 15 needles onto one spool of thread and puts a quilter's knot at the end. She pulls the length of thread she needs through the first needle, makes another knot, and cuts the thread. When she's out of thread in that needle, she simply repeats the process.

J.G., Salisbury, North Carolina

Recently I was machine quilting some mini-quilts for gifts and wanted to embellish the borders. I didn't have a seasonal stencil, so I used some of my cookie cutters to create quilting designs. I rubbed a piece of chalk along the lower edge of the cookie cutter to outline the edge. Then I stamped a temporary design onto the quilt.

L.C., Lindsay, Nebraska

I like to use fat quarters because I can have a variety of colors and fabrics easily at hand. Fat quarters are easy to organize because I just put them in baskets according to color and then put the baskets onto a bookshelf where they are easy to see. For lengths of fabric ½ yard (.50 m) or more, I fold the fabric in half lengthwise twice and then hang it on a hanger. Now I can choose my fabric and lay it on the cutting mat, ready for cutting. I no longer have to fold and press the fabric at the last minute, matching selvage edges and fighting the bulk of fabric. It is always pre-folded and ready to use.

R.S., Longview, Washington

Stitch Along the Paper

FOR AN EFFICIENT AND ACCURATE WAY TO MACHINE-QUILT INTERESTING GEOMETRIC DESIGNS, USE GRIDDED PAPER AS A GUIDE. MAKE ONE OR MORE QUILT BLOCKS THAT FEATURE THESE QUILTING DESIGNS; THEN JOIN THE BLOCKS WITH AN EASY QUILT-AS-YOU-GO TECHNIQUE.

STRAIGHT-STITCH TECHNIQUES

1. Cut the desired number of 9" to 12" (23 cm to 30.5 cm) squares of top fabric, batting, and backing fabrics. Pin the layers together.

2. Select a geometric shape. Mark the design on the gridded side of Grid Works™ Craft & Pattern Paper. Cut out the design shape *(Diagram A)*.

Note from Nancy: Grid Works has a special waxy coating on the non-gridded side that bonds temporarily to fabric without leaving a residue. Grid Works can be peeled away, repositioned, and reused up to 12 times.

3. Using a warm iron, press the wax-coated side of Grid Works to the right side of the quilt sandwich *(Diagram B)*.

4. Use Grid Works as a stitching guide. Stitch along the edge of the paper template; do not stitch through the paper.

5. Peel off, reposition, and press the paper to the fabric to guide the next row of stitching *(Diagram C)*.

6. Experiment with various stitching designs. Use the following designs as a starting point and then create additional patterns of your own. The suggested dimensions are only guidelines; feel free to adjust the size.

• Flame design: Make the design ½" wide by 1½" to 2" long (1.3 cm wide by 3.8 cm to 5 cm long) *(Diagram D)*.

• Step design: Make the steps 2" wide by 4" long (5 cm wide by 10 cm long) *(Diagram E)*.

• Wave or shell design: Use a cup or a half circle to shape the design.
– Position an outward scallop for the first row *(Diagram F)*.
– For subsequent rows, position the tip of each wave in the center of the wave of the previous row *(Diagram G)*.

• Try to preplan the designs so that

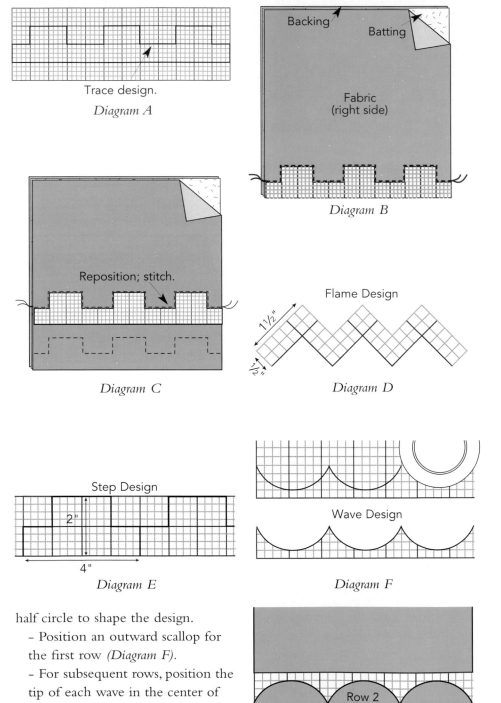

Trace design.
Diagram A

Backing Batting
Fabric (right side)
Diagram B

Reposition; stitch.
Diagram C

Flame Design
1½" ½"
Diagram D

Step Design
2" 4"
Diagram E

Wave Design
Diagram F

Row 2 Row 1
Diagram G

the machine quilting ends ¼" (0.6 cm) from the cut edges of the quilt block. This gives a finished look to the block when edges are joined in ¼" (0.6 cm) seams. It also makes it possible to trim some of the batting from that ¼" (0.6 cm) seam area, reducing bulk.

CONTINUOUS SCALLOP QUILTING

Secure the layers of your quilt by framing the quilt blocks with this attractive machine-quilted accent. Press-on templates, easily made at home, are the key to this scallop quilting design.

1. Create scalloped press-on templates.

• Measure the size of the completed quilt block *(Diagram H)*. If the blocks are separated by sashing, do not include the sashing.

• On a piece of gridded wax-backed paper, such as Grid Works, mark a line equal to the length of the measured block. Or as an alternative, draw a line that length on a piece of freezer paper.

• Place a circular object, such as a plate, a saucer, or an embroidery hoop, between the marks at the beginning and the end of that line. Draw an arc or a scallop *(Diagram I)*.

• Draw a mirror image of that arc or scallop on the opposite side of the

line *(Diagram J)*.

• Draw a series of identical scallops on the paper; cut them out. Cut each scallop in half along the original traced line.

2. Layer and pin the quilt layers as detailed on pages 126 and 127. Roll the quilt from the right to the left, leaving the first vertical row visible. Secure the rolled fabric with quilt clamps (such as Jaws™) or pins.

3. Press the scallop templates to the quilt top.

• Start at the upper left corner. Position a template, wax side down, along the top edge of the block, from corner to corner. Press the template in place.

$\longrightarrow$

Measure block.

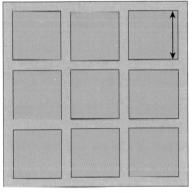

Diagram H

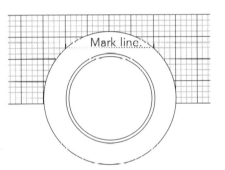
Mark line

Diagram I

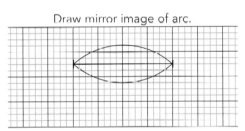
Draw mirror image of arc.

Diagram J

• Position and press templates on each side of the first vertical seam. Note that the templates do not extend into the frame or the sashing around the quilt block *(Diagram K)*.

4. Set up the machine as detailed on page 128. Use an open toe foot for greater visibility, insert a machine quilting needle, and thread both the top and the bobbin of the machine with cotton quilting thread. Or use monofilament thread on the top of the machine if desired.

5. Stitch the first section.

• Begin at the upper left corner. Lock stitches as detailed on page 129. Then change to a regular stitch length and sew along the edge of the press-on template. At the end of the first template, stop with the needle in the down position if possible. Pivot and stitch along the next template *(Diagram L)*.

> *Note from Nancy:* Because you need to roll the entire quilt to one side when you begin stitching, there will be a lot of fabric in the center of the machine. Because of this bulk, this technique may be better suited for small quilts than for large projects.

• Continue stitching along all templates to the left of the vertical seam.
• If the quilt blocks include frames or sashing, straightstitch between the end of one template and the beginning of the next *(Diagram M)*.
• At the end of the vertical seam, pivot and stitch along all the templates on the opposite side of that vertical seam, following the same technique *(Diagram N)*.
• After stitching along both sides of the first vertical seam, reposition the templates to stitch the next section *(Diagram O)*.
  - Remove the templates. Release

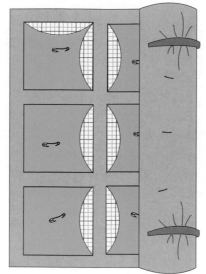

Position templates.

Diagram K

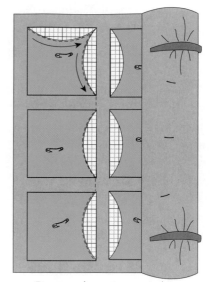

Pivot and continue stitching.

Diagram L

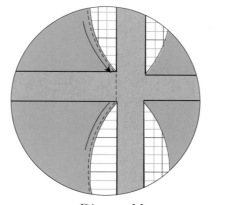

Diagram M

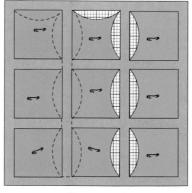

Diagram N

Diagram O

the rolled section to expose the second vertical row of the quilt.
  - Reposition the press-on templates along the next vertical seam, pressing with a dry iron. It may be necessary to roll the left side of the

quilt toward the second vertical row to make it easier to handle the quilt.
  - Stitch along the template edges up and down the second vertical seam.

- Repeat the process on all inner seams.
- Stitch the final scallop along the top edge, ending at Point A *(Diagram P)*.
- Turn the quilt 90° so that Point A (the upper right corner) becomes the new upper left corner. Continue as detailed above. Repeat the process until the entire quilt is scallop-stitched *(Diagram Q)*.

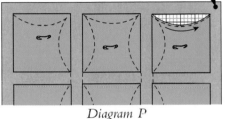

Diagram P

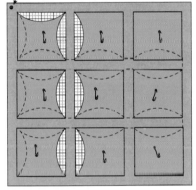

Diagram Q

Hanging Sleeve

A SLEEVE SEWN ON THE BACK MAKES DISPLAYING YOUR QUILT EASY. A DOWEL OR A CURTAIN ROD SLIPPED THROUGH THE SLEEVE CAN HANG FROM BRACKETS ON THE WALL.

Refer to *Hanging Sleeve Diagram* throughout.

1. Cut a 9½"-wide (24.3 cm-wide) piece of fabric that measures the width of the quilt plus 2" (5 cm). Turn under ¼" (0.6 cm) and hem on each end. Press and then turn under 1" (2.5 cm) more. Press and topstitch.

2. With the wrong sides facing, join the long edges. Press the seam allowance open, centering the seam on one side of the tube. With the seam facing the quilt backing, center the sleeve just below the binding at the top of the quilt.

3. Slipstitch the top and bottom edges of the sleeve to the quilt backing only. Do not stitch through to the quilt top.

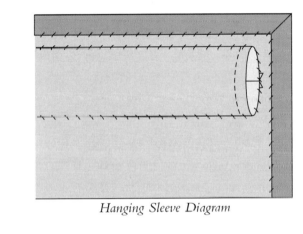

Hanging Sleeve Diagram

Straight-Grain Binding

STRAIGHT-GRAIN BINDING IS EASY TO MAKE AND TO APPLY.
IT CAN ALSO HELP YOUR QUILT HANG STRAIGHTER.

MAKING BINDING

1. Cut the number of 2¼"-wide (5.6 cm-wide) strips needed to bind the quilt.

2. Join the strips end to end to make one continuous strip. To join two strips, layer them perpendicular to each other, with the right sides facing. Stitch a diagonal seam across the strips *(Diagram A)*. Trim the seam allowances to ¼" (0.6 cm) and press open.

3. Fold the binding in half, with the wrong sides facing, along the length of the strip. Press.

APPLYING BINDING

Machine-stitch the binding to the front of your quilt first. Begin stitching in the middle of any quilt side. Do not trim the excess batting and backing until after you machine-stitch the binding to the quilt.

1. Matching raw edges, lay the binding on the quilt. Fold down the top corner of the binding at a 45° angle, align the raw edges, and pin *(Diagram B)*.

2. Beginning at the folded end, stitch the binding to the quilt, using a ¼" (0.6 cm) seam allowance. Stop stitching ¼" (0.6 cm) from the corner and backstitch. Remove your quilt from the machine.

3. Fold the binding strip straight up, away from the quilt, to make a 45° angle *(Diagram C)*.

4. Fold the binding straight down along the next side to be stitched, creating a fold that is even with the raw edge of the previously stitched line *(Diagram D)*.

5. Begin stitching ¼" from the top edge of the new side. Stitch along this side *(Diagram D)*. Continue until all four corners and sides are joined.

FINISHING BINDING

1. Overlap the ends of the binding over the beginning fold and stitch about 2" (5 cm) beyond it. Trim any excess binding.

2. Trim the excess batting and backing.

3. Turn the binding over the raw edges of the quilt and slipstitch in place on the backing, using thread that matches the binding *(Diagram E)*. Or stitch in-the-ditch from the right side.

4. At each corner, fold the binding to form a miter. Stitch the miters closed.

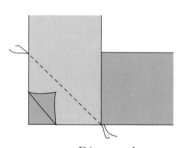

Diagram A

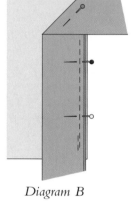

Diagram B

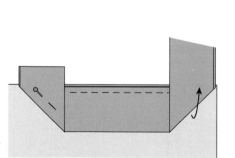

Diagram C

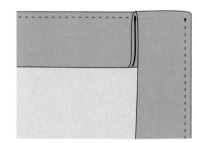

Diagram D

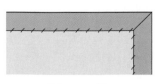

Diagram E

Bias Binding

SINCE BIAS BINDING HAS A LOT OF "GIVE," YOU MAY WANT TO USE STRAIGHT-GRAIN BINDING FOR MOST OF YOUR QUILTS. HOWEVER, YOU SHOULD USE BIAS BINDING WHEN YOU HAVE ROUNDED CORNERS ON A QUILT OR WHEN YOU WANT A PLAID BINDING ON POINT.

1. To cut bias binding, start with a square. (For a queen-size quilt, a 32" [81.5 cm] square is sufficient, so you should never need more than one yard of fabric.) At the top and bottom edges, center pins with heads toward the **inside;** at each side, center the pins with heads toward the **outside** edges *(Diagram A).*

2. Cut the square in half diagonally to make two triangles *(Diagram B).*

3. With the right sides facing, match the edges with the pin heads pointed to the **outside.** Remove the pins and join the triangles with a ¼" (0.6 cm) seam *(Diagram C).* Press the seam open.

4. On the wrong side of the fabric, mark the cutting lines parallel to the long edges. For most quilts, you'll want a 2¼" wide (5.6 cm-wide) binding strip. Draw lines 2¼" (5.6 cm) apart *(Diagram D).*

5. With the right sides facing, match the edges with the pin heads pointed toward the **inside,** offsetting one width of the binding strip. Join the edges with a ¼" (0.6 cm) seam to make a tube *(Diagram E).* Press the seam open.

6. Begin cutting at the extended edge. Follow the drawn lines, rolling the tube as you cut until all the fabric is cut into one continuous strip *(Diagram F).*

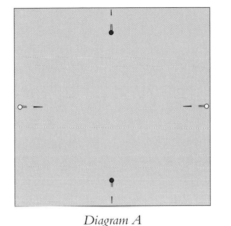

Diagram A

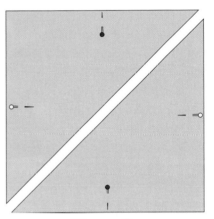

Diagram B

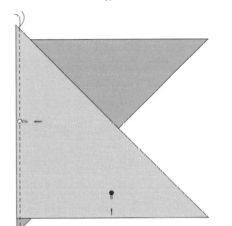

Diagram C

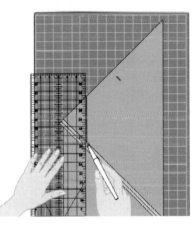

Diagram D

Diagram E

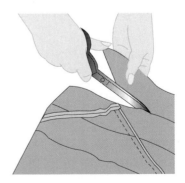

Diagram F

Quilt Labels

ONCE YOUR QUILT IS FINISHED, YOU'LL WANT TO ADD A QUILT
LABEL TO THE BACK SO THAT FUTURE GENERATIONS WILL KNOW
BASIC INFORMATION ABOUT THE QUILT AND ITS MAKER.

WHY A LABEL?

Labels serve a dual function:
They can be both informative and
attractive. For example, add a label to:
• Record important information,
such as who made a quilt, when and
where it was made, and for what
occasion.
• Provide instructions on how to
care for the quilt.
• Identify where the pattern came
from or if it was an original design.
• Serve as a loving reminder of the
person who made a handcrafted gift.

MATERIALS

Lightweight light-colored fabric
Pigma Micron Permanent Pens

DRAWING LABELS

1. Prepare the label fabric.
• Choose a 100%-cotton fabric or a
cotton/polyester blend. Inks tend to
bleed more with synthetic fibers.
• Prewash the fabric to eliminate siz-
ing that might act as a barrier to ink
absorption.
• Before you make your label, always
test the pen by drawing on a fabric
scrap. Pens react differently to every
fabric.
2. Draw your label design on the
nonwaxy side of a piece of freezer
paper cut slightly smaller than the
finished label. If the design includes
letters or one-way designs, reverse
the design and trace a mirror image
so that the design will appear correctly on the completed label. Use
one of our designs or draw your own

design. Use black ink to make the
design more visible during tracing.
3. Transfer the design to the label
fabric.
• Center the wax-coated side of the
freezer paper on the wrong side of
the fabric. Press in place.
• For the easiest tracing, place the
design and the fabric on a light table.
As an option, use a brightly lit window. Or if your dining room table has
removable leaves, open the table and
cover the opening with a piece of glass
or Plexiglas™. Place a lamp under the
opening to provide the needed light.
• Trace the design, using a Pigma
pen. Pigma ink is waterproof and
acid free. Pens come in various sizes;

the lower the number, the finer the
point. Trace slowly, taking time to
trace each section of the design.
• Let the ink dry thoroughly.
Remove the freezer paper.
4. Turn under the raw edges of the
completed label. Stitch the label onto
the back corner of your quilt.

SCANNING OR PHOTOCOPYING LABELS

You may want to duplicate one of the
quilt labels on the following pages. If so,
scan the quilt label into your computer
or make a color copy. Follow the instructions for photo transfer quilts on
pages 88 and 89 to use these designs.

*If you own a home com-
puter, try using it to print
designs on your blocks
and quilt labels. If you
don't like your handwrit-
ing, or if you just want
to add some creative let-
tering or clip art, your
computer will have a
wide variety of fonts and
images from which to
choose.*

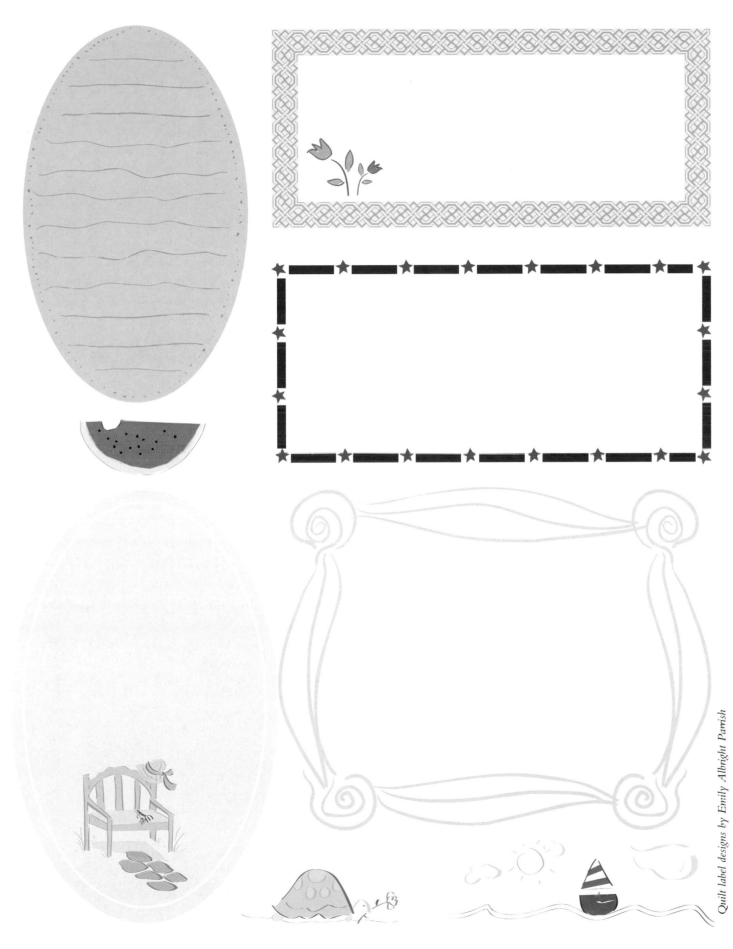

Quilt label designs by Emily Albright Parrish

Resources

CONTACT THE FOLLOWING COMPANIES FOR CATALOGS OR PRODUCT INFORMATION.

GENERAL SUPPLIES

Nancy's Notions
333 Beichl Avenue
P.O. Box 683
Beaver Dam, WI 53916-0683
1-800-833-0690
Web site: www.nancysnotions.com

HAND-DYED FABRICS

Alaska Dyeworks
300 West Swanson, #106
Wasilla, AK 99654
1-800-478-1755
E-mail: akdye@akdye.com
Web site: www.akdye.com

Fabrics to Dye For
85 Beach Street
Building C
Westerly, RI 02891
1-888-322-1319
E-mail: DYEfor@Riconnect.com
Web site: www.FabricsToDyeFor.com

KALEIDOSCOPE RULER

Doheny Publications, Inc.
P.O. Box 1175
Edmonds, WA 98020
1-425-774-3761
E-mail: orders@dohenybooks.com
Web site: www.dohenybooks.com

PFAFF

www.sewingstore.com

PROFESSIONAL MACHINE QUILTING

New Traditions Machine Quilting
Lena Colley
906 Catherine Street
Birmingham, AL 35215
1-205-833-0631
E-mail: Newtrad@aol.com